THE
ANDREASSON
AFFAIR

THE
ANDREASSON
AFFAIR

THE TRUE STORY
of a
CLOSE ENCOUNTER of the FOURTH KIND

By

RAYMOND E. FOWLER

Foreword by J. Allen Hynek

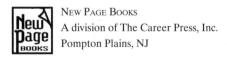
NEW PAGE BOOKS
A division of The Career Press, Inc.
Pompton Plains, NJ

THE ANDREASSON AFFAIR
EDITED BY JODI BRANDON
TYPESET BY EILEEN MUNSON
Cover design by Howard Grossman/12E Design
Printed in the U.S.A.

Transcripts of hypnotic and debriefing sessions © 1978 Raymond E. Fowler, Joseph Santangelo, and Fred R. Youngren.

Excerpts from UFO Report No. CE111/MA-77 (67-41a), "A Close Encounter of the Third Kind: UFO Report Involving Betty Andreasson and Her Family," © 1978 Raymond E. Fowler and Fred R. Youngren. All rights reserved.

To order this title, please call toll-free 1-800-CAREER-1 (NJ and Canada: 201-848-0310) to order using VISA or MasterCard, or for further information on books from Career Press.

The Career Press, Inc.
220 West Parkway, Unit 12
Pompton Plains, NJ 07444
www.careerpress.com
www.newpagebooks.com

Library of Congress Cataloging-in-Publication Data

Fowler, Raymond E., 1933-
  The Andreasson affair : the true story of a close encounter of the fourth kind / by Raymond E. Fowler ; foreword by J. Allen Hynek.
     pages cm
  Includes bibliographical references and index.
  ISBN 978-1-60163-346-0 -- ISBN 978-1-60163-440-5 (ebook) 1. Alien abduction. 2. Luca, Betty A. (Betty Andreasson), 1937- I. Title.

 BF2050.F678 2014
 001.942--dc23

                    2014021301

Also by the Author

*Dedicated to the
memory of Betty Andreasson's father,
Waino W. Aho,
and of her two sons,
Todd and James Andreasson, Jr.*

Raymond E. Fowler

﹥ Acknowledgments ﹤

Harold Edelstein, Joseph Santangelo, Jules Vaillancourt, David Webb, and Fred Youngren, for their direct participation in the investigation, and for providing significant data for use in this book.

Ernest C. Reid, for providing his services as Psychological Stress Evaluator Analyst.

Faith Youngren, who, with her father, Fred Youngren, developed the clay bust of Quazgaa shown.

Waino Aho, Eva Aho, and Rebecca Anderson, for their cooperation during the investigation.

Michael Andolina, George J. Bethoney, Susan Caddy, Nancy McLaughlin, Eugene Mallove, Peter Neurath, Virginia Neurath, Joseph Nyman, Merlyn Sheehan, Joan Thompson, Debbie Vaillancourt, Janet Walbridge, Evelyn M. Youngren, William Zarr, and the psychiatrist (who has requested anonymity), for providing valuable services to the investigators.

George Briggs, Gary Lehman, and Frank Pechulis, for reading and commenting on the manuscript.

Special acknowledgments to Dr. J. Allen Hynek for his kindness in providing the Foreword to this book; and to my dear wife, Margaret, who spent many hours proofreading the manuscript and providing encouragement when needed most.

⊱ Contents ⊰

➤ Foreword ◄

The UFO phenomenon, in its totality, is surprisingly complex. Understandably, this is not recognized by the general public. Although various opinion polls indicate that the majority of the population feel that "UFOs are for real," only patient study, and—even more important—direct involvement with the witnesses to this greatly perplexing phenomenon can demonstrate the extent of the complexity. The man on the street's simple opinion that either UFOs are all nonsense or that visitors from outer space do exist is brutally destroyed by close study. But this is not a new insight: In science, it is well recognized that investigations into many subjects spawn more questions than they answer. In the area of UFOs, deeper acquaintance reveals a subject that has not only potentially important scientific aspects but sociological, psychological, and even theological aspects as well.

The Andreasson case involves all these aspects—so much so, and in such bizarre fashion, that in the past I frankly would not have touched an invitation to write the foreword for a book treating "contactees," abduction, mental telepathy, mystical symbolism, and physical contact and examination by "aliens." But across the years I have learned to broaden my view of the entire UFO phenomenon, and I now realize that it is a composite of many "inputs." It does not seem to be just one single thing, but—as has often happened in science—what at first seemed to have just one component has turned out to have several.

This book really started with a letter to me from the principal witness. At that time I had neither the spare hours nor, I confess, the inclination to follow it up, and I let the letter lie for some time. Then one day I reread it. Here was a sincere person asking assistance, not knowing where to turn, and I felt I could not be callous and consign the long-unanswered letter to the "circular file." It occurred to me that because Ray Fowler and his associates were not too far from the witness, they might do the Center for UFO Studies and me a favor and discharge the obligation that the letter implicitly imposed. I am glad that Mr. Fowler undertook what at first must have seemed an unwelcome task. But he and his associates did, and there has resulted a most interesting book. No, "interesting" is not sufficient; it is a book that will captivate, bother, intrigue, and even frighten as one pursues it and contemplates its implications.

Fowler is to be complimented on his perseverance in the investigation of this case of very high "strangeness." It leads down many paths that make Alice's wanderings in Wonderland pale by comparison. And those who still hold that the entire subject of UFOs is nonsense will be sorely challenged if they have the courage to take an honest look at the present book. For whatever the UFO phenomenon is (or are), it is not nonsense. It would take an imagination of the highest order to explain the reported happenings described herein as mere misidentifications of balloons, aircraft, meteors, or planets! Neither is there the slightest evidence of hoax or contrivance.

The present work will also challenge those who consider UFOs solely synonymous with physical craft that transport flesh-and-blood denizens from distant solar systems. A former book by Mr. Fowler, *UFOs: Interplanetary Visitors,* upholds this more popular concept of UFOs, and many of the cases he describes tend to give strong support to that hypothesis. But here we have "creatures of light" who find walls no obstacle to free passage into rooms and who find no difficulty in exerting uncanny control over the witnesses' minds. If this represents an advanced technology, then it must incorporate the paranormal just as our own incorporates transistors and computers. Somehow, "they" have mastered the puzzle of mind over matter.

Of course, all this is predicated on the premise that this entire series of adventures is not the result of some complex psychological drama played in concert. If so, it would still be a fine case study in abnormal psychology. But more and more of these high-strangeness cases are surfacing. Like the Andreasson case, they outrage our common sense, and they do constitute a challenge to our present belief systems. Readers who become intrigued by the Andreasson narrative would be well advised to acquaint themselves with accounts of other Close Encounters of the Fourth Kind—not only those in which regressive hypnosis is the chief source of information, as in the present case. One can dismiss the hypnosis reports as unreliable and fanciful, but this is much more difficult to do where the data source is the witnesses' conscious mind. Such information is available through serious UFO organizations like MUFON (Mutual UFO Network) in Seguin, Texas, of which Mr. Fowler is one of the directors, and CUFOS (Center for UFO Studies) in Evanston, Illinois.

Readers who delve further into the fascinating world of the UFO phenomenon will come to understand for themselves the worldwide scope of the phenomenon, and the problems and challenges that it presents.

J. Allen Hynek
Northwestern University
Evanston, Illinois

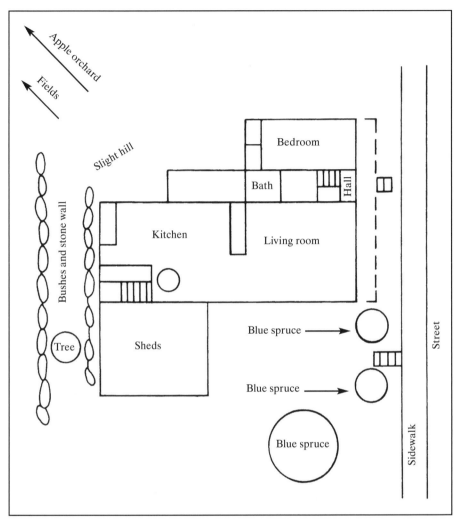

Figure 1: *The Andreasson house and property as they appeared in 1967.*

> Prologue to the Incredible <

In retrospect, Betty Ann Andreasson considered herself something of a tomboy. The minute she arrived home from school, she'd change clothes and head for pond or brook, field or wood, of rural Massachusetts. "I'd stick my feet in the pond edge or walk through the brook's thick mud. Every season felt so alive to me. I felt as if I was part of it. Even now, I feel total recall. The joy of standing by the cool rushing stream, with soft white dew-covered flowers, and skunk cabbage clustered in the swamp close-by." Betty loved to feast on wild blackberries, blueberries, plums, hazelnuts, and elderberries. "I used to climb large hemlock trees and pick lady's slippers, jack-in-the-pulpit, trilliums, mountain laurel. I would go deep into the woods and stay almost 'til dark. I was never afraid there. It was so peaceful."

At 17 she became engaged to James Andreasson, 21, who had been in the Navy for four years. They were married on June 13, 1954, in Fitchburg. A year later, their first child, Becky, was born, and six other children followed swiftly after.

Finding a house to accommodate their family had been no easy task. Finally they bought a "handyman special," for no money down, in South Ashburnham, a small town in northern Massachusetts. James, although a pipe fitter by trade, used his natural expertise in carpentry to make the former farmhouse comfortable for the bustling family. They tore down a crumbling wraparound porch and repainted the walls inside and out. (See Figure 1 on page 19.)

South Ashburnham is typical of many New England towns. Rolling wooded hills and bordering lakes have gradually surrendered to the Cape Cod houses, ranches, and mobile homes that have usurped their territory, but remnants of a once-active farming community are still evident. Abandoned orchards, tottering barns, and ivy-covered, gray stone walls all bear silent witness to another day. The Andreasson children—Becky, age 11; James, age 10; Mark, age 9; Scott, age 7; Todd, age 6; Bonnie, age 4; and Cindy, age 3—became accustomed to the neighborhood, enjoying the company of their newfound friends.

Secure in her vibrant Christian faith that had grown stronger over the years, Betty sought to instill the same faith and ideals within her own family. Each Sunday, Betty marshaled her well-scrubbed children to the local community church. "The house and yard were always filled with children. We would sing songs and tell stories from the Bible and have fresh-baked cookies and milk."

But 1966 had been a disrupted Christmas for the Andreasson family, and prospects for the new year of 1967 did not look bright. On December 23, two days before Christmas, a woman had pulled out of a blind side street and collided with the rear of James's gray Volkswagen sedan, sending him into a head-on collision with an oncoming automobile. Severely injured in the crash, James would need weeks in intensive care in the hospital, followed by months in traction.

Eleven-year-old Becky was a great help to her mother in dealing with the many needs of her younger brothers and sisters. But with the prospects of James Andreasson being hospitalized for many months and of Betty being faced with a host of responsibilities her husband had usually shouldered, extra help was desperately needed. Such were the circumstances that prompted Betty's parents to join the busy household to lend a helping hand.

Betty's father, Waino Aho, had immigrated from Finland as a young child when his family, seeking better opportunities in the United States, bought and worked a dairy farm in Massachusetts. Later, while on Army leave from Fort Devens, Massachusetts, Waino had met his future wife, Eva, a native New Englander. Betty was the second-to-youngest of Aho's five offspring.

By mid-January, Betty's own seven children had become used to a new schedule of early suppers, designed to allow their mother a nightly visit with her husband at the local hospital. January 25 was one of those days when the warm promise of spring hung dreamily in the air. The snow that had blanketed the ground for more than a month had all but vanished. Much later, under hypnosis, Becky would recall that on that balmy afternoon, she and her girlfriend had been playing in the nearby orchard. They were climbing one of the apple trees when her mother's call to supper echoed up into the orchard.

About an hour later, after eating and helping with the dishes, Becky went out again. But now, as the last vestiges of daylight melted into the darkness, the mild temperature of the afternoon dropped rapidly, and Becky soon returned inside. Already pools of mist were beginning to collect in the hollows around the old farmhouse, bringing the promise of a foggy night.

As on most evenings, James, Jr., Mark, Scott, Todd, and Bonnie had all been fed and dressed for bed and were watching television—on this evening, Bozo the Clown. Three-year-old Cindy was curled up on her grandmother's lap. Betty was in the kitchen, finishing up a few remaining chores.

Suddenly the electric lights began to flicker hesitantly and then blinked out, throwing the house into darkness and confusion, and sending frightened children scurrying into the kitchen to find their mother. Almost at the same time, the family saw a curious pink light shining through the kitchen window

Ten years later, under hypnosis, Betty and Becky Andreasson would describe the scene as follows:

Betty: Suddenly the lights were off, and we wondered: What was it?
And we looked over and there was a—by the window, the small
kitchen window—I can see like a light, sort of pink right now.
And now the light is getting brighter. It's reddish-orange, and
it's pulsating. I said to the children, "Be quiet, and quick, get
in the living room, and whatever it is will go away." It seemed
like the whole house had a vacuum over it. Like stillness all
around—like stillness.

Becky: The next thing I knew, Mom was going, "Shhh! Be quiet!"
There's some huge pulsating glow that was out in the kitchen. It
was outside. Like a big glow!

The Andreasson kitchen had become a kaleidoscope of reflected
color and dancing shadows keeping cadence with the flashing light. As the
frightened Betty herded her excited children back into the living room,
Betty's father hurried into the kitchen to see what was going on. Glancing
into the backyard through the pantry window, Waino Aho stared out in
disbelief.

What he saw is best described in his own signed statement. Despite the
shaky handwriting, the old man's words carry a ring of conviction that is at
odds with their bizarre import:

*These creatures that I saw through the window of Betty's house were
just like Halloween freaks. I thought they had put on a funny kind of
headdress imitating a moon man. It was funny the way they jumped
one after the other—just like grasshoppers. When they saw me looking at them, they stopped...the one in front looked at me and I felt
kind of queer. That's all I knew.*

The Andreasson Affair had begun.

This book you are about to read deals with what is known, in the ter-
minology of UFO investigators, as a CE-IV—a Close Encounter of the
Fourth Kind.

Close Encounters of the Third Kind, the title of the spectacular movie
about UFOs, is a designation originated by Dr. J. Allen Hynek to describe
specific types of UFO reports. In all, Dr. Hynek has coined six major
categories:

NL—Nocturnal Light: lights seen in the night sky

DD—Daylight Discs: distant disc-like objects seen during the day

RV—Radar/Visual: UFOs seen by radar and vision simultaneously

CE-I—Close Encounter of the First Kind: a UFO seen within 500 feet

CE-II—Close Encounter of the Second Kind: a CE-I that leaves physical traces

CE-III—Close Encounter of the Third Kind: a CE-I with humanoid occupants seen

The Andreasson Affair is more than just a classic example of a CE-IV, however. It is—again to use the jargon of the Ufologists—a case of such "high strangeness" that even the most open-minded investigators were at first inclined to dismiss it out of hand. Yet it has become probably the best documented case of its kind to date, the subject of an intensive 12-month investigation conducted for the Center for UFO Studies (CUFOS) that involved, among other things, the recording of large quantities of testimony given under hypnosis, extensive lie detector testing of witnesses, detailed analysis of corroborative circumstantial evidence, careful character checks (see Appendix A), exhaustive comparison with other CE-IV accounts, and much more.[1]

The results of this investigation filled three volumes of a 528-page confidential report. But even after our disbelief had given way under the sheer weight of the supporting evidence, there remained (and remains) some baffling problems of interpretation. At certain points, Betty's narrative seems to deal with a reality so alien that it can be described only in metaphors, and perhaps only understood in terms of an altered state of consciousness.

Because this book is also the story of how the Andreasson family's account was investigated and substantiated, perhaps I should begin by explaining how I, though skeptical at first, came to be involved.

My own interest in the whole phenomenon of UFOs dates back to the late 1940s, when I began collecting and studying everything I could about the subject before joining the Air Force in January 1952. Since I had an amateur radio license and obtained high scores in radio/electronics, the Air Force chose to send me to a special school involving electronic espionage, after which I was assigned to the United States Air Force Security Service under the auspices of the National Security Agency. My involvement brought me in contact with information that indicated that the military took UFOs very seriously indeed.

I was honorably discharged as an Airman First Class in December of 1955. In 1960 my continuing interest in UFOs prompted me to become an associate member of the National Investigations Committee on Aerial Phenomena (NICAP).[2] In 1963 I began conducting personal on-site inquiries into local UFO sightings, submitting written reports of my investigations to NICAP and to the U.S. Air Force on an unsolicited basis. Later, I became an official NICAP investigator and in November of 1964, became chairman of this group.

My report on a classical UFO sighting that took place at Exeter, New Hampshire, instigated John G. Fuller's well-known book *Incident at Exeter*[3] and became a major topic of discussion during the first open congressional hearings on UFOs in April 1966. In 1971 I became Massachusetts state director for an international group called the Mutual UFO Network (MUFON).[4] While remaining with NICAP as a consultant, I also became a scientific associate/investigator for the Center for UFO Studies, directed by Dr. J. Allen Hynek, who formerly had served the U.S. Air Force Projects Sign, Grudge, and Blue Book as chief astronomical consultant for about 20 years.

In 1975 MUFON appointed me as national director of investigations. One of my first tasks concerning this new assignment was to write and edit a detailed UFO investigators' field manual, which was published in 1975 and has since been adopted for use by the Center for UFO Studies and other groups abroad. The manual closely followed many of the investigative procedures recommended by Dr. Hynek.

Unfortunately, many sightings in all categories go unreported to official agencies. It is estimated that only 10 percent of all witnesses to UFO sightings ever file a report. And the stranger the experience, the less likely it will be reported. CE-IVs may be the key to the entire UFO mystery, but of all categories of reports, they are the most inherently unbelievable and the most difficult to verify. And to complicate the problem, the memories of witnesses to a CE-IV often seem to have suffered a strangely selective amnesia. In abduction cases particularly, most witnesses recollect only a close-up UFO sighting. A few may remember seeing alien creatures, but rarely do they recall many details. The actual contact or abduction experience has somehow been erased—perhaps mercifully so—from their conscious minds. Later, vague flashbacks, dreams, and intuitive feelings cause witnesses to suspect that something unusual has happened to them. And nonetheless, details of the abduction experience remain locked in the deepest recesses of their minds.

Where does someone go to report a UFO experience so bizarre that one hesitates to discuss it with either family or friends? Where does one turn when government officials have publicly decreed that UFOs do not exist? Such was the plight of the Andreasson family. During the following years, the hazy yet vivid experience had weighed heavily on the thoughts of Betty. Her daughter Becky thought it had been a bad dream, and yet it seemed so real. At times, Betty would receive mental flashbacks concerning the weird episode. Provocative insights and alien scenes surfaced momentarily from her subconscious, only to slip away as her conscious mind sought to retain them.

Thus in 1974, when the *National Enquirer* solicited firsthand UFO accounts for consideration by a panel of scientists, Betty was one of those who responded, hesitantly reporting the vague details that she remembered. Her reply was a form letter from the *Enquirer* expressing no interest in the incident, frustrating Betty's hopes of casting light on what had happened to her family.

Then in August 1975, she read an article about the Center for UFO Studies in a local newspaper. The news story reported that Center Director Dr. J. Allen Hynek was requesting UFO reports for scientific study. Betty sat down and penned a fateful letter, describing the sketchy details of what seemed to have been a CE-IV:

> To Dr. Hynek: August 20, 1975
>
> I am so happy to read someone is finally studying about UFOs. Now I can tell someone of...my experience...an encounter in 1967 with UFO occupants....

Dr. Hynek received Betty's letter and filed it for some months before resurrecting it and sending it to MUFON's Humanoid Study Group,[5] which had requested copies of all such CE-IV cases from the files of the Center for UFO Studies in order to prepare a computer-generated listing.

After some discussion, the study group decided that Mrs. Andreasson's account might be worth looking into. Because Betty's UFO experience had occurred in Massachusetts, the study group had asked MUFON investigators in that state to enquire into the case for them. In January 1977 Field Investigator Jules Vaillancourt initiated an investigation.

It soon became evident that to produce any meaningful results, we would have to be able to unlock whatever memories were still buried in Betty's and Becky's unconscious minds. We recalled that a similar problem had come up with the classic UFO abduction case involving Betty and Barney Hill that was described in John Fuller's *The Interrupted Journey*.[6] Although remembering an initial CE-IV, the Hills nevertheless could not account for a portion of time immediately afterward. It was recommended that they secure the services of a psychiatrist, Benjamin Simon, MD, and during the course of his treatment, Dr. Simon used hypnotic regression to help the Hills consciously recall the missing hours. A similar procedure seemed indicated for the Andreasson Affair.

Harold J. Edelstein, who directs the New England Institute of Hypnosis[7], is one of few persons who have pursued the art of hypnosis as a full-time career. Patients are referred to him from a number of local hospitals, including the Sydney Farber Cancer Center and the Massachusetts Rehabilitation Psychiatric Department. In addition to his work within the institute, he serves as staff member to Comprehensive Psychological Services (Burlington, Massachusetts) and as faculty instructor at three colleges, and also serves a number of law-enforcement agencies. Harold is, in short, a well-recognized expert in the practical use of hypnosis.

He became involved as a consultant in UFO research through the influence of one of our MUFON investigators, Merlyn Sheehan. (While being treated for cancer at the New England Baptist Hospital, Merlyn's doctor referred her to Dr. Edelstein to relieve the nauseating side effects of chemotherapy treatments.) Though this was Harold's first experience with a UFO investigation, his warm personality and keen insight into human behavior soon enabled him to establish complete trust on the part of Becky and Betty—no simple task, as both women initially had severe misgivings about hypnosis.

Both Betty and Becky were good subjects, and after a few sessions, it would only take a few minutes to put either of them in a deep trance. Dr. Edelstein feels it would be unethical to describe in a book for general readers the exact methodology that he used to induce hypnosis. I can report, however, that he employed such devices as key words and slight pressure with his hands. (I remember that he once pointed his finger at Betty to show us her reaction: She went out like a light, and her body went limp like a rag doll.) During deep trance hypnotic regression sessions, Betty and Becky relived their traumatic experience in great detail. They each expressed natural apprehension, fear, wonder, concern, pain, and joy. Their facial expressions, voice tones, and tears were obviously genuine.

The MUFON state director, Joseph Santangelo, kept me abreast of developments. Initially skeptical, I nonetheless was curious and listened carefully to tapes made of the hypnosis/debriefing session. It soon became apparent to me that both witnesses were wholly sincere. When preliminary lie detector tests indicated that the witnesses were indeed telling the truth, I joined the team as a principal investigator and began attending sessions on June 4, 1977.

If you belong to the majority of adult Americans that believes UFOs exist (nearly 57 percent according to a 1978 Gallup poll), you may find it easier to believe that Betty's story, though certainly fantastic, is not fanciful. But even if you belong to the still-skeptical minority, even though you may not share all of the conclusions we eventually drew from this investigation, I think you will find the evidence too substantial and compelling to be easily dismissed. Intricate elements of their story remained consistent over 12 months of cross-examinations. Subtle similarities with other reported CE-IVs added further corroboration. A rather unusual feature in this case is the abductee's artistic ability. When Betty attended Westminster Elementary School, art was her favorite subject after math and spelling, and she won first prize in many art contests. During our later investigation, she was able to provide detailed sketches relating to her experience, some depicting the interior of the UFO. In combination, these sketches produced powerful corroboration of her account of her experience.

Much of this book consists of actual transcribed words of the hypnotized witnesses as they related and relived their CE-IV to my colleagues and me. Other than editorial comments provided for clarity and organization, most of the account is taken directly from the transcribed hypnotic regression sessions—which have been rearranged so as to provide a strictly chronological sequence of the original experience.

Is the story of the Andreasson Affair true? For now, at least, each reader must draw his own conclusions—until the time when an even more substantial CE-IV casts a more definitive light on Betty's experience. You may find the account incredible and even incomprehensible in parts. But one thing has been established beyond the shadow of a doubt: The witnesses believed it happened.

And so, for that matter, do I.

C·H·A·P·T·E·R 2

≻ Uninvited Visitors ≺

When the bright light first flashed through the kitchen window, Becky had returned into the living room in response to her mother's commands. (See Figure 2 shown on page 32.) Looking down the hallway into the kitchen, she noticed a dark silhouetted shape bobbing in front of the light source shining through the kitchen window. Then, everything went black. At that same moment, Becky, her grandfather, and all family members except Betty found themselves unable to move, unaware of anything else.

In the pages that follow, I will let the witnesses tell their story themselves.

Jules: (investigator) What's happening, Betty?

Betty: There's some...the lights are back on now and, ah, there are *beings* standing there and they're talking with me, but not with their mouths. They've got big heads!

Joseph: (investigator) How did they get there, Betty?

Betty: They came through the door.

Joseph: Did you open the door for them?

Betty: No.

Joseph: Did *they* open the door?

Betty: No.

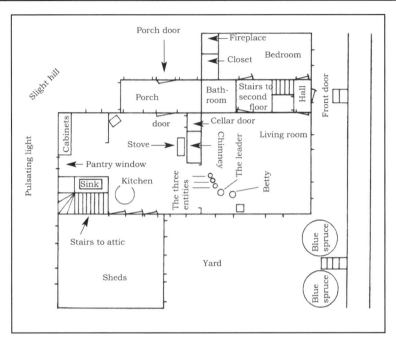

Figure 2: *The ground floor of the Andreasson house at the time of the encounter.*

The four entities that had passed by the window entered the house by going through the kitchen door—not through the frame, but through the kitchen door itself. They passed through its solid wood as if it were nonexistent.

Betty: They came in like follow-the-leader.... They are starting to come through the door now...right through the wood, one right after the other. It's amazing! Coming through! And I stood back a little. Was it real? And they are coming, one after another.... Now they are all inside.

It was difficult for us to visualize what Betty was describing. Thus, after each session, Dr. Edelstein induced a posthypnotic suggestion within her that she would remember the details of what she described while under hypnosis. Her ability to draw was fully utilized, and she supplied us with detailed pencil sketches, many of which are reproduced in this book. (See Figure 3.)

Betty: I was wondering. How did they ever do that? How did they get in here like that?

Betty balked, as her mind frantically tried to grasp some logical explanation for what was happening. Then her strong Christian beliefs abruptly surfaced to provide a desperately sought rationale.

Figure 3: *Betty's rendition of how the entities appeared through the closed kitchen door. They "moved in a jerky motion, leaving a vapory image behind." Drawn April 10, 1977.*

Betty: I'm thinking they must be angels, because Jesus was able to walk through doors and walls and walk on water. Must be angels.... And Scriptures keep coming into my mind where it says, "Entertain the stranger, for it may be *angels unaware*."

Although Betty is far from being fanatic in her beliefs, her pronounced fundamentalist Christian orientation undoubtedly colored her perception and interpretation of some of the events that befell her.

The four entities hardly resembled conventional depictions of angels. They were identical, except for the leader, who appeared taller. The creatures had gray skins, and large, outsized pear-shaped heads. Their faces were mongoloid in appearance.

Betty: And the taller one...his eye seems to...his left eye seems to quickly go up into a slit. [See Figure 4 shown on page 34.]

Large, wraparound catlike eyes stood in stark contrast to less prominent facial features: holes for noses and ears, and fixed, scarlike mouths. They wore shiny dark blue, form-fitting uniforms. Each left sleeve was adorned with an emblem that resembled a bird with outstretched wings. (See Figure 5.) Their three-digited hands were gloved (See Figure 6), and they wore high shoes or boots.

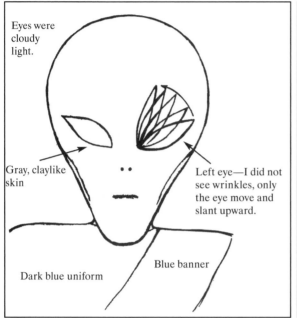

Figure 4: *The leader, as he appeared in the kitchen (May 18).*

Figure 5: *An Entity in profile.*

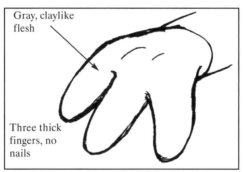

Figure 6: *April 9.*

Betty stood transfixed. But an extraordinary calm settled over her. An aura of friendliness emanated from the alien intruders, and she was no longer frightened. The leader, who stood about four feet tall, identified himself as "Quazgaa."[1]

Harold: (hypnotist) Did they know your name?

Betty: Yes, he called me Betty. It seemed like an oral sound but it...it—ah, I think it was a transformation of thought but it seemed like an oral sound.

During the initial establishment of what seems to have been mental telepathy, Betty misconceived a mental impression generated by Quazgaa. The leader stretched out his hand, and she asked, "Do you want something to eat?" They merely nodded.

Betty: And so I went and got some food from the refrigerator and a pan from the stove, and I started to cook some meat.

The entities stared impassively at Betty momentarily, and then she received another mental impression.

Betty: And I turned, because they said something to me. And they said, "We cannot eat food unless it is burned." And so I started to burn the meat—and they stepped back, astonished over the smoke that was coming up!

The beings corrected Betty as clearer images formed in her mind:

Betty: And they said, "But that's not our kind of food. Our food is tried by fire, knowledge tried by fire. Do you have any food like that?"

Betty's religious beliefs influenced her reply: "Yes, I think I have some like that...it's in there."

The events that followed in rapid succession are utterly alien to the logical model of reality that we have been taught since early childhood. Like a computer that is automatically programmed to reject extraneous data, the human mind rejects such claims with the comfortable labels of hoax, dream, or hallucination.

Betty: They followed me into the living room, and I looked and I saw all my family *as if time had stopped for them.* And I wondered what happened. But I glanced down and picked up the Bible that was on the end table. I turned and I passed it to the leader. The leader passed me a little thin blue book in exchange. [See Figure 7 on page 36.]

The entity who called himself Quazgaa took the Bible from her and held it in his hand. Betty's mind rebelled at what occurred next, because what she saw happen seemed impossible.

Betty: The leader put the book [the Bible] in his hand... [*sigh*] And he waved his hand over it, and other Bibles appeared, *thicker* than the original. Then he passed it to those beside him and they took the books and each one was spontaneous. They somehow flipped it, page by page, and looked down. Each page was pure white, luminous white. And then they stopped—and I started to look in the little blue book.

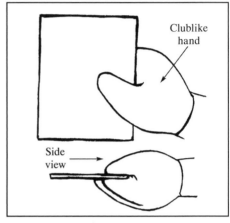

Figure 7: *April 9.*

When Betty's oldest daughter, Becky, relived the episode under hypnosis, she recalled regaining consciousness at this very point. After blacking out, the next thing she remembered was seeing her mother conversing with the entities in the corner of the living room.

Jules: Where are you? In the hallway?

Betty: I'm in the living room still...I'm over near the TV, and I'm just looking over to the left.

Jules: What do you see?

Becky: Some...I don't even know what it is! There's something there, and it looks so scary. But Mom's okay.

It was very unsettling watching and hearing Becky during the hypnotic session. Now, years after the event, a mature 22-year-old adult reclined in the hypnotist's chair. But the voice coming from her mouth was that of an 11-year-old child!

Joseph: Is this "something" one thing or many things?

Becky: It's...it looks like it's a clay man. He looks like a—a clay man... talking to my mom. Some kind of man-creature. And behind him, right behind him toward the right, there's one, a little one—and there are two after him that are just exactly like triplets.

Joseph: How do you know they're men?

Becky: I don't know. They just seem like men to me. They're men. They're really babies, but to me, I guess, they would be more man than woman. They look like clay. They look like they're smooth, watered-on clay.

Jules: Did they touch you?

Becky: No, they didn't touch me.

Jules: Did they take you outside?

Becky: No, they didn't take me outside or anything. They didn't even—I was standing right there watching them, and they knew I was standing right there watching them, and they knew that my other brothers...my brothers and my—wait a minute. My one, two, three brothers were sitting there, and Grammie—she's over there...Oh! Where's Grampy?

Jules: He was with Grammie, right? You can't find Grampy?

Becky: No, I can't see Grampy there.

Jules: Is Grampy in the kitchen?

Becky: No, he's not. No one's in the kitchen. Grampy went out to look with Mom—he's looking out the window.

Little Becky was visibly upset. When she awoke briefly from suspended animation, her grandfather had seemingly disappeared. In reality, he had gone to look at the flashing lights—first out the kitchen window and then out the pantry window. At the time Becky was looking for him, he was standing in suspended animation in the pantry, out of her sight.

Joseph: Did your mother give anything to the beings?

Becky: I don't know. My mom was standing there with her hand on something, and that clay form had his hand on the other part, like a book...the clay hand is holding it on the right-hand side, and Mom is standing on the...

Joseph: Where did the book come from?

Becky: The book? I don't know. She must have had it—I don't know.

Becky had not seen the aliens enter the room with her mother. She had not witnessed the amazing duplication of the Bible, nor did she see them give her mother the blue book. When Becky regained consciousness, the first thing she noticed was her mother looking at the blue book with Quazgaa.

Becky: I woke up and they were in the room...Mom was talking to them, and there was a book already in his hand.

Jules: Is the TV off?

Becky: Yes, the TV—no, the TV is...it's different. No picture, no sound—very, very dim like you turn down the color—like you turned it down so it's very gray and low.

Throughout the sessions, when Betty or Becky became anxious during certain segments of their experience, Dr. Edelstein reassured them. He sensed their particular needs instinctively at the right time and in a correct manner. The confidence and the precision with which he controlled the situation were most impressive.

Harold: Becky, you are upset about something, aren't you?

Becky: Yes!

Harold: What are you upset about?

Becky: Those things. They're scary.

Harold: They're scary? But you told us that once before you felt a very, very close relationship to them—that you like them.

Becky: Yes. They are very kind, and they don't mean any harm, but they are scary to look at...they look scary.

Harold: They look scary? Okay, I want you to realize that you went through all of this—without any harm befalling you. Is that right?

Becky: Yes.

Harold: Therefore, you have nothing to fear. Just relax...just relax.

Becky was asked to describe the beings in detail.

Becky: They were wearing...it looked like pants and a tucked-in type of shirt, but it was tight-fitted. Something like a—what it reminded me of was something like a scuba diving outfit that would be close to a person's skin.

Joseph: Where did the bottom of the legs of the skin suit...where did they end?

Becky: They ended near the shoe.

Joseph: Could you see the bottom of it? Did it continue right around the foot?

Becky: Yes, the bottom of it. The bottom of the first one had—like his pants went down like a skin suit, and then there was a cut where it was. It stopped with one lighter shade and it went into a darker shade...like a shoe or a boot would be.

Fred: (investigator) Could you describe their eyes?

Becky: They looked like marbles.... It had big eyes.

Jules: What about the eye slit? Did you see that move at all?

Becky: No, I didn't see anything—like him closing his eyes or opening them.

Fred: Did they have ears?

Becky: I can't see it.

Fred: Did they have hair on their heads?

Becky: No, I didn't see any hair. His head looked like a pear, an upside-down pear.

Fred: Did he have nostrils?

Becky: I didn't even see a nose, so I don't know.

Fred: A mouth?

Becky: Sideways he didn't have a mouth. When he turned, he did. It was like a *wrinkle* in the clay—not a line, but like a line. And I can't see any nose. I see—there's a lot of shadow around. The only thing I can see really good was the big...eyes. Like marbles. They looked scary.

Harold: Sleep for a moment. Just relax, relax, relax. Deeper and deeper.

Jules: Are you afraid?

Becky: Yeah, I'm afraid because he scares me by the way he looks, but I can't do anything—can't move. I'm not afraid of him, because there's a feeling that he's not going to hurt me. He scares me just by the way he looks.

Becky watched her mother and the little men as they looked at the small blue book.

Becky: That book. It was bright, and Mom was thanking them for something, and so it must have been the blue book....

Instinctively, the taller entity became aware that Becky was awake.

Betty: The head, the tallest one looked right around across where the kids were and Gram was, right over to me, and then he stopped when he saw me standing there. And then he went from me, right back around, and started talking or looking at Mom. And then, all I can see is nothing but darkness—then nothing.

At that point, Becky lapsed back into unconsciousness. Let us return to Betty's vantage point, as she examines the little blue book with the alien visitors:

Betty: ...I started to look in the little blue book. And the first three pages were snow white, luminous white. And I saw this silver gray top thing with, like coils—and there was sort of a wheel, and inside were four things. I can't make out what these things are...and so I've come to the close of that book—closed it.

When Betty closed the book, the eyes of the entities focused on hers.

Betty: And their eyes are so funny. One minute they are light, and now they've got a black ball in it. And they move straight, especially that left eye and...

Betty had sought desperately to break through the strange tranquilizing effect that somehow shielded her mind from the reality of what was happening. She succeeded momentarily, and reported the following exchange:

"What are you doing here?" Betty asked.

"We have come to help," the entities replied. "Will you help us?"

"How can I help?"

"Would you follow us?" the entities asked.

"Are you of God?" she demanded. "You keep saying you have come to help the world. Why?"

"Because the world is trying to destroy itself," they answered her. "How can I help the world?" she sighed.

"Would you follow us?"

"If you are of God," Betty sighed again. "If you are here to help and are of God, I would follow, but do not deceive me."

"Would you follow us?" they repeated.

Betty's power to resist lessened as the entities stared hypnotically into her eyes. Their slow, repetitive invitation, "Would you follow us?" echoed within the deepest recesses of her mind. But again, her own powerful instincts surfaced: "What about my children? My parents?"

"They are all right," Quazgaa answered. "Would you follow us?"

Jules: What was the rest of your family doing?

Betty: They promised me they wouldn't hurt them—that they would be all right. They said, "See, they're just resting there." There was no fear on their faces. It was as if they were unaware.... They said, "They are all right. Would you follow us?" He keeps on repeating that—"Would you follow us?"

"Oh, Lord," Betty said softly, "show me what I'm supposed to do."

"We will not harm you." The entities repeated, "Would you follow us?"

"All right," Betty replied, very softly.

C•H•A•P•T•E•R 3

➤ On Board ≺

Betty: He said, "Stand directly in back of me." And so I stood in back of him, and I swooped in somehow, like suction. And immediately, when I did, he was starting out the door, and I was going *through* the same thing, the wood, that they were.

Joseph: Nobody opened any door?

Betty: No. I was right in their line. I was following the leader, and I guess they must have—ah, their line must have a passage through.

Betty was no longer walking. She found herself floating several inches above the ground with a swooping motion that matched the movements of her abductors as they moved along together in single file.

Betty: I'm just swooping along, step by step as he moves. I'm moving the exact distance from him. The others evidently are following.

Peculiar foreign sensations pulsed through Betty's body.

Betty: My legs feel very strange. My whole body does. It feels like it's weightless...very funny. And we are outside, and he stopped.

Betty stared in disbelief. In her backyard, resting on its own struts, was an oval object with a raised central portion. This concerned the investigators. How could such a remarkable object remain undetected by the neighbors? We interrupted Betty to ask pertinent questions.

Ray: How about the other houses? Could you see the neighborhood?

Betty: No. I saw haze, all haze.

Ray: When you went out, how do you know that you were actually in the neighborhood?

Betty: I didn't know except for the corner of the house and the ship. The rest of the part seemed very vague and hazy—like a mist was all around.

During the course of our investigation, the present owner of the house confirmed that the low area in the backyard is especially conducive to dense pockets of fog. Weather records for the night of January 25, 1967, indicated heavy mist in the area.

Debbie: (Jules's wife) How about the garage?

Betty: I couldn't see that, and I couldn't see the opposite side of the house on this side.... I could just see on this left-hand side, the house, the corner of the house, the stone wall, and the tree. Even past that, it seemed misty. It seemed as if the ship took up most of the area, too much for me to see past it.

Betty stood awestruck at the silent presence of the strange craft in the yard. Her initial shock quickly gave way to fear and apprehension. Quazgaa seemed to have sensed this and, to reassure Betty, did a remarkable thing.

Betty: He says, "See, you can trust me. Look over at the ship." And he made the bottom like glass. I could see through it!

When the bottom of the craft suddenly became transparent, Betty recognized some of the things inside, which she had seen illustrated in the blue book.

Betty: I see the—part of those things I saw in the book. There are glass balls on the bottom, cut glass like, and there are arms that come down and grasp on to it, and they go up.... And there's that thing on the side. And they can rotate on an inner tube—with that gray matter and that water, I guess, or something. [See Figure 8.]

Betty sought in vain to find a comparative reference point to describe what she was observing. "What is it?" she breathed. "What is it, Quazgaa?

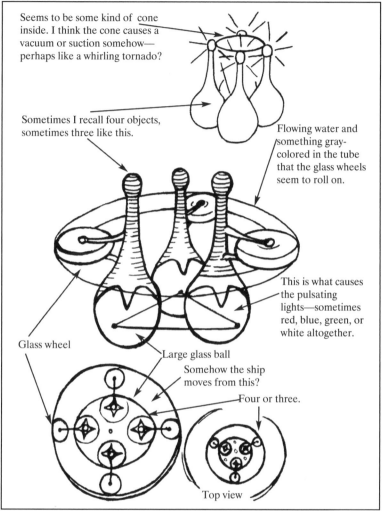

Seems to be some kind of cone inside. I think the cone causes a vacuum or suction somehow—perhaps like a whirling tornado?

Sometimes I recall four objects, sometimes three like this.

Flowing water and something gray-colored in the tube that the glass wheels seem to roll on.

This is what causes the pulsating lights—sometimes red, blue, green, or white altogether.

Glass wheel

Large glass ball

Somehow the ship moves from this?

Four or three.

Top view

Figure 8: *Apparatus in the bottom of the craft. May 5.*

"I have other things to show you," he replied. "Come along, come along."

Betty: And the ship turned back so that it was not glass but like a... silver-gold. And I see the legs, and they are parked, sort of, on the hill.

In other words, the length of the vehicle's legs on struts were adjusted to the incline of the hill adjoining the backyard. (See Figure 9 on page 46.) Quazgaa faced the alien vehicle and raised his left hand. Instantaneously an opening appeared in the craft.

Betty: And, ah, that door is opening—automatically, I guess, or else he's making it. He raised his hand. And we are getting all lined up. And he swoops right up! There are three stairs. Soon as he goes up, I'm swooped up, and the others are following.

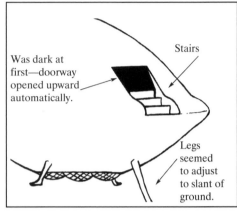

Figure 9: *The craft's exterior. May 7.*

Betty found herself floating into a small room with curved walls. The door closed automatically behind them.

Betty: We're in like a half-bubble, or quarter of a bubble, room. And he [Quazgaa] has withdrawn himself with the others, and they are standing over there talking.... [See Figure 10.] I'm just looking at this room. Something goes down on the sides of the

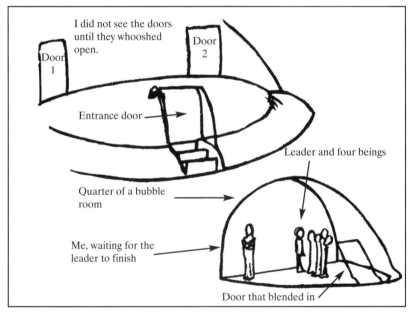

Figure 10: *The entrance hall. May 7.*

bubble.... Where the steps come up, it goes down.... I feel very weightless and icky. My hands and my legs feel like they are asleep or something. And they are still talking over there, and they glance over at me once in a while.... Oh, hurry up! And I'm crossing my arms now. I'm tired of just standing there.... I feel weightless. Oh, my feet are pins and needles or something— even my arms and my hands. He's still talking, and...about two or three of them are leaving. That door whooshed open, and they are going in—and it's closing.

Then Quazgaa came over to Betty. Two entities still remained in the room and stood watching her.

Betty: ...He brought me over to where they were, and...he is saying something to them about going and making himself ready. [*Sigh.*] Would they please bring me to the upper room?

Betty and the entities left; Quazgaa stayed behind.

Betty: And so, the two—one went in front of me and one in back of me, and we went over to the furthest right-hand end of the quarter bubble. And whoosh! Another door opened. And you can't even see those doors. They just go up when they open. And there are stairs there—going around, somehow going around. They seem like they are floating up, but...my waist feels so heavy there. And we are going up those stairs. Looks like I can see something down there. We're all going around the stairs and...we are going up around, and this door goes down. [See Figure 11 on page 48.]

At this point, the hypnotist turned over the recording tape.

Harold: Betty, I now want you—to just remember where you are. You said, "This door leads down."

When she was asked to continue her account, Betty quickly corrected him:

Betty: The door *goes* down. It doesn't *lead* down. It disappears down somehow. And now they are going into that room.

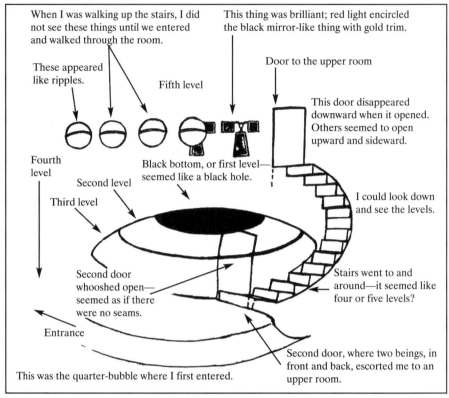

When I was walking up the stairs, I did not see these things until we entered and walked through the room.

This thing was brilliant; red light encircled the black mirror-like thing with gold trim.

These appeared like ripples.

Fifth level

Door to the upper room

This door disappeared downward when it opened. Others seemed to open upward and sideward.

Fourth level

Second level

Third level

Black bottom, or first level— seemed like a black hole.

I could look down and see the levels.

Second door whooshed open— seemed as if there were no seams.

Stairs went to and around—it seemed like four or five levels?

Entrance

This was the quarter-bubble where I first entered.

Second door, where two beings, in front and back, escorted me to an upper room.

Figure 11: *Interior of the craft. May 25.*

Betty, still positioned between the two silent beings, was perplexed at what she saw as she moved into a circular room.

Betty: I see that—ah, box, or that desk and, ah, see something else. It's, ah, red and black. It's black, outlined with red. And it's some kind of mirrors, I think. [*Softly*] I don't know. Seems like there are, ah, in that circular room, big ripples like windows. [See Figure 12.] They are leading me still [*sigh*] and they are bringing me over to that further edge—are bringing me further over there. And now they're stopping and I'm standing there.... And the two are withdrawing. They are saying that I'll be all right here for a time.

"How come I have to stay here?" she asked them. An unseen force held Betty firmly in place. Paralyzed except for head movement, she felt deserted and helpless. As she relived the episode, we saw the terror reflected on her face before us. Her pulse quickened, and the hypnotist quickly reacted.

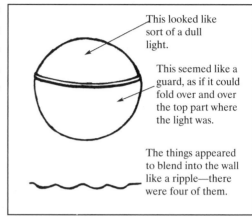

This looked like sort of a dull light.

This seemed like a guard, as if it could fold over and over the top part where the light was.

The things appeared to blend into the wall like a ripple—there were four of them.

Harold: Betty? This is Dr. Edelstein. Just relax. Are you getting apprehensive right now?

Figure 12: *The "ripple-like" windows. May 5.*

Betty: They are leaving me alone in there!

At times, Dr. Edelstein suggested that he was *with* the witnesses to give them moral support.

Harold: All right, Betty, just relax. This is me. I want you now to feel myself being with you to back you up. You've got nothing to fear. You can feel the fear leaving you, can't you? I'm by your side constantly. Continue—go ahead. You have nothing to fear.

Now substantially calmed, Betty tried to describe a variety of totally alien objects that she could see from her vantage point. But their utter strangeness prohibited her from describing them except by comparing them with things already familiar to her.

Betty: Okay, I'm standing there and looking around on the side, there—on the wall, there is a leaf motif, and, ah, there's a thing up top there, like a—it looks like a railing, but it isn't. And the room is sort of dome-shaped...there are leaf motifs to the right there...raised buttons on it, and there are shields...and different symbols—and the desk is to the side and...and—I don't like feeling so held down in my body. I just seem to be able to move my head to look. They seem like they've controlled my body somehow so I'm fixed, like in one place, and, ah...

Harold: Are you becoming apprehensive?

Betty: No.

Harold: Fine, I'm still with you.

Betty: Can *you* see the things?

Harold: No, I can see them only through your eyes. Continue.

Betty: I'm trying to see what else is there. I can't see way in back of me. There are those golden, ah, those golden things—the cord and, um, some type of a scroll.

Betty, in the meantime, had waited impatiently and wondered what fate had in store for her when the alien beings returned.

Betty: I wish they'd hurry up. I'm tired of waiting here. It's getting brighter. They are getting it brighter now in here.... [*Softly*] What is that? I see something like a—wonder if it's coming from the wall or is—what?... They've opened something, pushed it out, and it's something like a camera works. [See Figure 13.] [*Softly*] I don't know what it is, but it's getting brighter in here—uh, much brighter now. What's that? There's somebody coming now for me. They said, "Would you follow me, please?" And they stopped in front of me.

Harold: Betty, is this Quazgaa who is telling you this?

Betty: No.

Harold: All right, I want you now to lock this point in your mind. Lock this point, and when we start next time, you will carry on from this point in time. You will remember where you left off. Do you understand what I'm saying to you?

Betty: Yes.

Harold: You will store this particular spot in your subconscious mind, and when we start the next time, you will start from here and continue to go further.

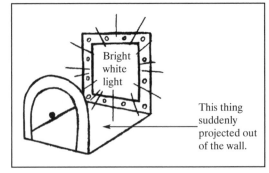

Figure 13: *May 5.*

At this point, Betty recovered from hypnotic trance.

The investigators awaited each following session with burning curiosity. What would happen next? But two weeks passed before we met again with the witnesses in the offices of the New England Institute of Hypnosis.

It was a hot, sultry June day. The steady drone of an air conditioner pervaded the otherwise-silent atmosphere that soon enveloped the room as Dr. Edelstein prefaced the session by speaking into an activated tape recorder.

Harold: Today's date is the fourth of June 1977. The time is 12:21. This is a continuation of the session we made two weeks ago. Betty, I want you now to induce hypnosis into yourself. Very good. Now deepen this hypnosis by relaxing. Let yourself relax. Let yourself relax. When I touch your shoulder, let yourself go into the deepest point of relaxation you have ever been. Deeper and deeper—deep, deep, relaxation. I want you now to take yourself back to the last session that we had. You will go back to that point. Tell me you are there. Are you there now? Fine! I want you to continue.

We were amazed at how, week after week, the witnesses would pick up their accounts at the precise point where Dr. Edelstein had left off on the week before. Deep trance hypnosis, properly administered by a skillful hypnotist, can produce near-total recall of everything a subject has ever experienced. In this trance state, a person must tell the truth, as he or she believes the truth to be. Betty and Becky were turned off and on like biological tape recorders! It was fascinating to see a practical demonstration of the mind's remarkable facilities for storing memory.

Betty: The lights are getting brighter, and—that door opened again. And there is somebody coming. I'm glad they are coming, 'cause it seemed like a long time in there.... They're sort of gliding toward me, not moving their legs, but gliding. And it's one of the beings, ah, it's two of the beings. They are waving their hands and telling me to follow them. I'm going over with them.... And, ah, they are taking me over to the center of the room. One is in back of me

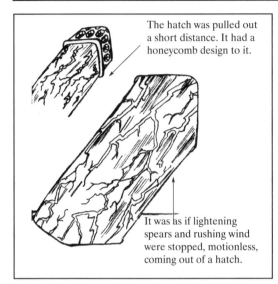

The hatch was pulled out a short distance. It had a honeycomb design to it.

It was as if lightening spears and rushing wind were stopped, motionless, coming out of a hatch.

Figure 14: *Lightning and rushing wind from the hatch. June 17.*

and one is in front of me. I asked them, "Where are we going now?"... And they said, "You will come over here." I went over to the center of the room, and I stood there. And the one in front of me turned and looked at me.

Again, Betty was instructed to assume the familiar follow-the-leader stance between the two entities. Abruptly, she found herself sinking through an opening in the floor.

Betty: I'm standing there, and we are slowly, slowly being lowered through a tube. It looks like a—silvery tube... slowly lowering down. We are going down...we are going down. We are stopping. And one of the beings tells me to get in back of him again. I'm getting in back of him, and the other one's in front of me. And the door is lifting up—couldn't see the door before. The door just looked like a tube—clear, straight-through tube. I'm going out into another room that looks—looks like a hatch or something on top there. Looks like lightning spears coming out of it. [See Figure 14.] I don't know what it is, but it is there, and they are bringing me over to the side.

The rectangular construction that Betty referred to as a "hatch" looked similar in appearance (but not in size) to the enclosed walkways employed at airports between terminal gates and parked aircraft. Its surface was marked with both jagged and straight lines, which looked to Betty like graphic representations for wind and lightning. At this time, the hatch extended downward out of the wall and into the floor.

When Betty returned through this room later, the hatch had been tele-scoped into the wall, revealing an opening in the floor over which it had extended.

Next, Betty was directed to a platform illuminated from above by streaks of dazzling light. (See Figure 15.)

Betty: I'm seeing this brighter light shining down, and it—it's shining down so much, it's leaving like, ah, thin, tiny bars of light, surrounding it—like you do in a cartoon with a light bulb... having streaks of light from it, coming down.

"Would you get under that, please?" the entities asked.

"Well, what is it first?" Betty asked.

"It is just a cleansing thing."

"Well, will it hurt?"

"No," the entities replied. "It is just to cleanse you."

Betty: And so they didn't touch me, but they held out their hands as if to assist me. There seems to be a platform there [*sigh*], and I'm stepping on the platform. The light's above there. And it's bright—bright, and it's got those streaks of light coming out of it. It seems like it's moving me upward!

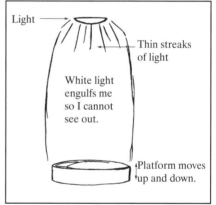

Figure 15: *The cleansing device. June 17.*

The platform itself moved upward and immersed Betty in the brilliant light.

Betty: The light is getting brighter and brighter. It's all engulfed in light—like I'm engulfed in light. I don't know if there is a covering or what, but I can't seem to see them. It's just bright white light.... I'm just standing there. It doesn't seem to hurt. It is not hot. It's just white light all around me, and on me. And now it is going back down. The platform is going back down...it is stopping....

Betty stepped off it, and the entities said, "Would you follow us, please? Now!"

"Where are we going now?" she asked. "Just please follow with us."

Betty: They motioned again for me to get to the back of them and follow the leader.... And he walked to another place where a door is opening—whooshing open.

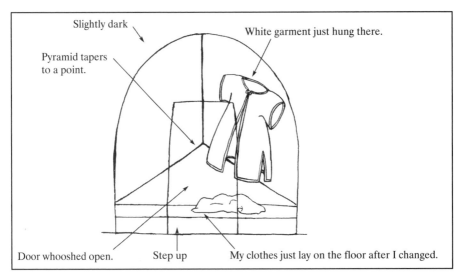

Figure 16: *The changing room. June 17.*

Betty faced the opening to a darkened wedge-shaped room. (See Figure 16.) The lead entity gestured, holding out his hand for her to enter. "It was a little bit dark in there," Betty recalled.

"Would you please change?" the entity said.

"I don't want to change!" she protested.

"Please! Would you just please change?"

"But why do I have to change?" Betty persisted.

"There's a white garment there for you," the entity said. "Would you please get into it?"

Now Betty bridled. "Look, I came here of my free will. Why do I have to change into this now?"

"Please change. Quazgaa is waiting for you."

"I want to talk to him!"

"Please change," the entity repeated. His persistent request drummed in Betty's ears until she finally relented. The white garment hung without visible support in the changing room.

Betty: And he kept on motioning to go into that room. It was kind of dark. I didn't like it. And so I said, "All right." And I had to step up into that room too. And I'm in that room and it's all—it looks like a pyramid on its side with a bubble where you went into the door.... Just enough standing room.... There—there's that white garment there.

Betty's modesty clearly manifested itself as she timidly removed her clothes.

Betty: And so I took off the first thing of my clothing, and I wondered if they've got something looking in there. And so I took that white garment, and I put it around me while I took off the rest of my underthings. And I slipped into that white garment. [See Figure 17 on page 56.] And that white garment was open in the front...[*sigh*] and loose around the arms, and it went down to about my knees, and it was sealed around the edges somehow. It had sort of like a scoop neck thing. And it had a—like a silver clasp up at the top. It had slits on both sides and a little slit in the back. But the front was kind of wide open, so I sort of wrapped it around me. And I banged on the side there, and I said, "I'm ready!" And the door whooshed open again—went open somehow.

Outside the changing room, the entities awaited Betty. She became fearful and prayed frantically for help. "Ah," she thought to herself. "What is all this about? What are they going to do to me?... Oh, Jesus be with me!"

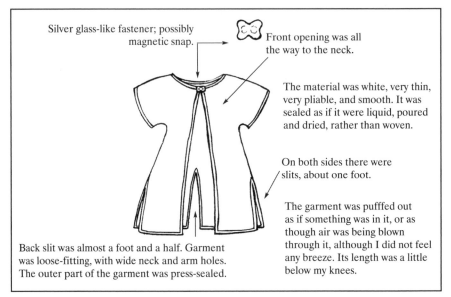

Silver glass-like fastener; possibly magnetic snap.

Front opening was all the way to the neck.

The material was white, very thin, very pliable, and smooth. It was sealed as if it were liquid, poured and dried, rather than woven.

On both sides there were slits, about one foot.

The garment was pufffed out as if something was in it, or as though air was being blown through it, although I did not feel any breeze. Its length was a little below my knees.

Back slit was almost a foot and a half. Garment was loose-fitting, with wide neck and arm holes. The outer part of the garment was press-sealed.

Figure 17: *The white examination garment. June 17.*

The entity nearest the door seemed to sense Betty's fear.

Betty: When I said that, that leader glanced at me quickly—sort of surprised or stunned. I guess he was reading what my thoughts were, and he seemed to move a little slower. I guess he saw that I was wondering what this was all about, 'cause he said, "You'll be all right. Follow us. Please get in back of me again." He seemed a little concerned, because he kept looking back checking to see if I was getting in back. And the other one just quickly got in back of me and we started off again. It seemed we were just gliding along on rollers or something or other. He came to the wall and he just stopped, and the door opened....

C•H•A•P•T•E•R 4

> The Examination <

Betty found herself entering a brightly lit room. (See Figure 18 on page 58.) We asked her to describe it to us.

Fred: How large is the room?

Betty: Very large. Very high over my head. Very wide, but it closes in on you.

Fred: Does it have corners?

Betty: No, it's dome-shaped. It's rounded.

Jules: Can you see the source of the illumination?

Betty: It comes from all over the place.

Jules: Is the ship moving?

Betty: I don't feel as if it's moving. I couldn't tell—because I'm just in that room, that building, or whatever it is.

Jules: Can you see any furniture?

Betty: Yes. There's something like a desk or boxlike thing.

Jules: Can you see any welded seams on the wall or some type of seam?

Betty: No, it seems smooth all the way around...smooth.

Joseph: How did you gain access?

Betty: They put me in there.

Jules: How did the being touch you?

Betty: They didn't really touch me.... There was something that they had power that I *automatically* went.

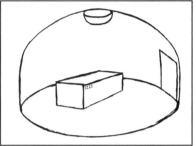

Figure 18: *The examination room. May 7.*

When Betty entered the hemispherical compartment, the first thing that caught her eye was an elongated desk or table. A closer look revealed what appeared to be a control panel on its side. It reminded her of an operating table, and she shuddered.

Betty: The two of them are there. And I see the table or that square thing, whatever it is, that's a—examining thing? "No! I don't want to get up there!" And on the side there are buttons. And that other one *glided* over to that other side there and..."I don't want to get up there!" And Quazgaa is coming in now, and he's in a different suit—with some others. And he comes over to me....

"You're going to be all right," Quazgaa said. "You are going to be okay."

Betty: And somehow they've got me—they are putting me on that flat center thing!

Harold: All right, fine. You will have no apprehension, because this was all in the past. Did they actually put you on the table to examine you, or did you get on the table?

Betty: No. It seemed like I *floated* up there somehow. I was just swept off my feet and laid there.

The alien creatures' physical examination of Betty was one of the most emotion-packed portions of the case. In the earlier hypnosis session devoted to this episode (on May 7, 1977), Betty was not allowed to relive this painful episode as a participant. Through hypnotic suggestion, she was removed from the role of active participant so that she could view the scene merely as an impassive observer.

Harold: All right, now, I want you to relax. You can feel yourself settling, still more and more. All right; you will have nothing to fear. Did they have to tie you down in order to perform the examination? [*Betty remained silent.*] Were you strapped down or were you held?

Betty: I was held somehow, because I didn't want that examination.

Harold: Fine. Just relax. Deeper and deeper.

Fred: Were the beings all of the same kind?

Betty: They were all the same kind, but one was taller than the others.

Fred: Were they dressed alike?

Betty: In that room, they seemed to be in different clothes—shiny white silver clothes. [See Figure 19 on page 60.]

Fred: Were these different beings than the ones you met in the kitchen?

Betty: Their skin seemed whiter. Maybe it's because of the bright light in there. It didn't seem so claylike gray.

Fred: The leader was the same as the one you had in the kitchen?

Betty: Yeah, he's the same.

Harold: What happened next?

Betty: There's a big block—long block-thing they had me on, and... lights coming from the walls, and...wires, *needle* wires. They took those long silver needles—they were bendable—and they stuck one up my nose and into my head!

Jules: Did you feel the pain?

Betty: Yes, but they touched the top of my head and took it away—touched my forehead. They said they were *awakening* something...

Harold: Just relax for a moment, okay? Just relax, relax, just relax. You're going deeper and deeper into a beautiful place of peace, of quiet—your whole body is relaxing as you go still deeper and deeper.... All right, continue now, Betty.

Joseph: Are there any sounds associated with this particular experience?

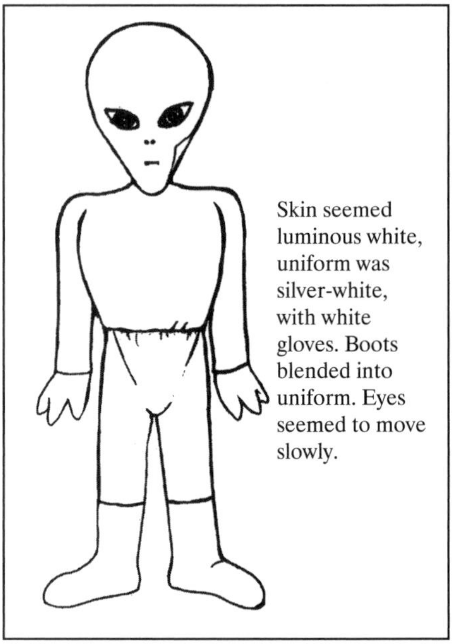

Betty: When they stuck that needle up my nose, I heard something break like a membrane or a veil or something—like a piece of tissue or something they broke through.

Skin seemed luminous white, uniform was silver-white, with white gloves. Boots blended into uniform. Eyes seemed to move slowly.

Jules: When this object was inserted in your nostril—was it a drilling effect, or just a penetrating?

Betty: Just a penetrating-pushing.

Jules: Which nostril?

Betty: My left...left.

Fred: Did they leave you alone for a while?

Figure 19: *The entities in the examination room. May 18.*

Betty: No. They were getting it over and done with. And they inserted another long silver thing through my belly button—my navel. And when they did, they started talking with each other.

Fred: What was this long thing connected to?

Betty: I really can't see it, 'cause I'm lying down straight.

Joseph: Did they tell you what the purpose was for the penetration of your navel? What was that examination for?

Betty: Something about *creation*, but they said there were some parts missing.

Joseph: Can you explain to us what was meant?

Betty: It was because I had a hysterectomy, I guess.

Shortly after young Cindy's birth, Betty had had to enter the hospital for suspected cancer. The operation was even more complex because Betty was four months' pregnant. Because the state of her health would have precluded her carrying the baby to term, the surgeons performed a hysterectomy. (Happily, the operation was a success, and Betty soon returned home.)

Harold: Betty, just relax. I want you now to tell yourself within your mind exactly how you're going to feel when you awaken. And then awaken yourself, feeling exactly that way.

When Betty awakened from hypnosis, Harold asked her, "What do you think?"

"It's kind of unbelievable to me," she replied.

Later, at the June 4 session, it was decided to let Betty actually relive examination as a *participant*. We began at the point when Betty had been somehow swept off her feet into the air and slowly lowered onto the table.

"What are you going to do, Quazgaa?" she asked.

"Just want to measure you for light," Quazgaa said.

"That's what you are going to do? Just measure me for light?"

"We are just going to measure you for *light*."

Betty: And, ah, I'm lying there, and he, ah, has this thing—ah, two bars to the side, and like a fan and tulips on the end. [See Figure 20.] And, ah—[*long sigh*] I don't [*sigh*]...He's waving it over me, and, ah, he says...

"You have not understood the word that you have," Quazgaa told her. "You've misunderstood some places.... There are spots there from it.... You are not completely filled with the light."

"I believe I am filled with the light!" Betty strongly protested. "I believe—I believe that I'm filled with the light!"

"We will have to measure you physically," Quazgaa replied.

"You told me that I wouldn't have to be measured physically...that you have measured others in the past physically, but you wouldn't have to measure me because of the light."

"But we have to, because there are some spots there."

"Is this going to hurt?" Betty asked. "I thought that you would only measure me for light."

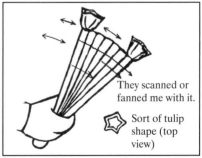

They scanned or fanned me with it.

Sort of tulip shape (top view)

Figure 20: *May 5.*

Betty: I feel shaky.... He's taking an instrument and—I'm going to stand
             over the [*sigh*]...I'm in complete control...control. He's taking an
             instrument and—ah-h-h-h!... Ow-wow!... [*Deep, fast breathing.*]
             Why do you have to put that up my nose—oh-h-h-h-!

Our hearts went out to Betty, as the face of the attractive, gentle
woman in the hypnotist's chair was alternately creased with expressions
of apprehension and pain. My hands gripped the notepad as I tried unsuccessfully to disassociate myself from the trauma being relived before
me. In her mind's eye, she was at that very moment held captive within a
strange craft, pinned upon a rectangular metal block, and staring up in
pain and raw terror at strange alien creatures, one of whom had pushed a
long silver needle into her left nostril. Her deep, heavy breathing continued, her face distorted in pain.

Betty: He's putting that thing in my nose, and it's going up and it's
             breaking through something. "I don't like it! Oh, and I can't
             move. It's hurting!" He has that thing up in my head. Oh-h-h-h!
             [*Her lips quiver.*]

At that point, Quazgaa apparently eased Betty's pain by placing his
hand on her forehead and on the top of her head. Betty's body relaxed no-
ticeably. "Thank you," she said softly.

At this juncture, Harold interrupted Betty's experience, feeling that
she had gone through enough anxiety and pain.

Harold: All right, I want you to open your hand. I am lifting it. You
             can feel me lifting it. I want you to feel the warmth of my hand
             entering your hand.

A sense of relief swept through his office. We all had had enough for
that day.

Harold: You can feel yourself relax—relax...I'm going to awaken you.
             At the count of three, you will awaken. You will feel completely
             relaxed. Your arms will move. You will feel completely relaxed.
             You will feel completely normal.... The next time I put you into
             hypnosis, you will immediately go to this point and go *from* this
             point still further. One—you are coming out of it...feeling better
             and better. Two—wide awake. Three!

Betty was allowed total recall of what had occurred under hypnosis. She was puzzled and wondered why she had not *relived* the experience the previous session on May 7.

"I didn't experience this when we *first* went through it," she said. "Why am I more shaky?"

"Because you went through a trauma now," Dr. Edelstein explained. "That's why I cut it short."

"But *before* when it came out, it..."

"Because you weren't reliving it," Harold said. "It was just something you were talking about."

We were very appreciative of Betty's cooperation. Recalling these strange happenings caused her much mental strain and anguish, and her conscious mind found it difficult to accommodate the weekly influx of once-forgotten terror. When she had sufficiently recovered the harrowing time in the hypnotist's chair, we initiated a period of intense debriefing.

Fred: At one point, you seemed to be trying to separate yourself from what was going on, trying to *stand off* to one side. Is that really what you were doing at that time?

Betty: No. I was on the table, and they had that long, thin needle and they were going to insert it in my nose—they told me they had to do that. And I was thinking of what Dr. Edelstein also had told me. For some reason, I still have the understanding, you know, of it...I was trying to separate myself from what they were going to do.

Joseph: This is when you were saying you were in complete control?

Betty: Yes, I was trying that, to see if I could get away from going into that—where they were going to use the needle.

Fred: But that didn't help you very much.

Betty: I *couldn't* separate from it, because I just felt as if they had some kind of magnetic thing holding my hands.

Harold: Feel her hands.

Ray: (author) Cold!

Harold: They *were* still colder than that.

Ray: Did you see anything that was strapping you down?

Betty: No. It just...they somehow had my hands—my legs and my hands.

Ray: Could you move your head? Could you move anything?

Betty: I don't think that I could turn my head.

Our questions continued late into the afternoon. Finally we returned to our homes, shocked and bewildered about what we had experienced that day. It would be another week before Betty was again hypnotically conveyed to the examination room of the alien craft, but it was decided that at the next session we would allow Betty to continue reliving the physical examination as a participant.

Our Saturday hypnosis sessions had by now become quite routine. That day, however, we were so eager to get started that the customary rendezvous at a local pancake house and the drive to Harold's offices seemed like hurdles in a race.

Investigators tensed and recorder switches clicked as Harold Edelstein's familiar preamble set the stage for session number nine. "This is June the 19th, 1977...."

Betty lay back comfortably in the plush reclining chair. Feeling that she had to know what had happened to her, she was determined to find out the truth. In a very short time, Betty was deeply under the influence of Harold's soft but firm voice. "Deeper and deeper...let yourself go. Deeper and deeper." Soon her body was perfectly relaxed. Her face was a picture of serenity. In several minutes, she would be spirited away to another place at another time where things had not been so peaceful.

Fred: Betty, we would like to go back to when you were in the craft. You are in the room, and they are starting to measure you physically.

At first, Betty started out impassively, describing what was happening from an onlooker's vantage point.

Betty: Yes, I'm—they have that—they have put it up inside of my head. I was feeling pain from the needle, and they put their hand on my forehead and on the top of my head, and it took some of the pain away. I don't know why they have to do that in the first place. I asked them, "Why do you have to do such a thing as this?" I still complained that they had said they were only going to have to measure me for light, and not this kind of test. And they said it's very important that they should do this. But they won't explain why.

And that other one is coming over by him with some kind of thing in his hand—looks sort of like a...paper, but it's like *webbed* paper or sort of a roll. [See Figure 21.] He opened it up a little bit to show him.... Quazgaa is looking at it.... They still have that thing stuck up my nose [*sigh*] and he's looking at the thing. They're pulling it out a little bit. Ah-h, makes me feel dizzy with that thing there. He's saying, "It's not going to be much longer." He's still looking at that weblike thing, whatever it is. And there's talking about something. He's pointing down at something.... And now the other man or that *being*—or whatever he is—is taking it and rolling it back up.... And he is turning to me.... They are going to take that thing out. I hope it doesn't hurt!

Her face became lined with fearful apprehension.

Betty: He's taking that thing out now.... Oh! It feels funny. [*Sigh*] They took it out, and it looks like *there is some kind of a ball on the end of it*—something on the end of it. A little thing, whatever it was, on the end of the needle. [See Figure 22 on page 66.] It's kind of hard to see what it is. [*Sigh*]

Betty described the needle as *removing* something from her nasal cavity. This was intriguing! Where had it come from? How did it get there? The atmosphere within the crowded office was charged with an air of expectancy. But because an interruption at that time was unthinkable, I made a note to inquire about it later. When the customary debriefing session began in earnest, I asked about the object which the aliens had removed through Betty's nose.

Ray: I was curious as regarding the *ball* on the end of the needle when they pulled it out of your nose.

Betty: It was a little *ball* with little prickly things on it.

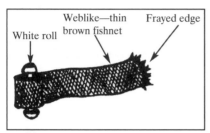

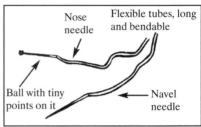

Figure 21   Figure 22

The needles used in the examination. June 19.

Ray: Was it there *before* they put it in your nose? Did you notice it?

Betty: No.

Ray: It wasn't there when they originally put the needle in your nose?

Betty: No.

Ray: You are fairly certain about that?

Betty: Yes.

Another interesting aspect requiring further clarification was the strip of webbed paper used in conjunction with the needle inserted in Betty's left nostril.

Ray: On that weblike paper. On the roll—did you notice any writing or markings on it at all, or was it clear?

Betty: It was weblike netting.

Harold: Like webbing on a chair? Is that what you mean? Like these chairs with the warp and the woof?

Betty: Yes. It was uniform all the way across. But it was not of that, uh, string material—it was brown. It was a tan brown. And it was spooled—from a little roll. It was pulled out, and it was frayed at the end. They were looking at it, and then they pulled it out further and pointed to something.

Fred: Did you see what they were pointing at?

Betty: It all looked the same.

After removing the needle from her nostril, the diminutive creatures huddled together as if discussing the results of measuring Betty physically. Betty watched in utter despair. She felt helpless, desolate, and cut off from all human help and compassion. Her captors exuded little emotion, moving and behaving with cool, dispassionate precision. Betty felt like a human guinea pig.

Betty: And now they are going over there and talking. [*Sigh*] Oh boy, I'll be glad when this is all over with! [*Sigh*] They are talking about something over there.... Now they are looking over at me. [*Sigh*] They are coming over again.... And they are saying they have to measure me for *procreation.*

Betty became terrified and cried out anxiously, "What are you doing that for? What is that?"

"It won't hurt," they said. "Don't worry, it won't hurt."

"I didn't think that other would hurt either," she retorted, "but it hurt!"

Now, under hypnosis, as Betty approached the next segment of the painful physical examination, she alternated back and forth between the roles of observer and participant:

Betty: And so, they are getting ready for something. They are down by my feet somewhere. They are doing something there. They are not touching me, but they are doing something.

Betty strained the movement of her eyes to see what the entities were doing. Her vision was restricted because she could not lift her head.

Betty: It must be something down there they are preparing. I can't see it.... Now they are pulling something. That needle again with a tube, like on the end. They are pulling—looks like he's pulling.... Oh! And he's opening up that shirt, and—he's going to put that in my navel! Oh-h-h-h. I don't like this!

As I leaned closer to Betty, a wave of empathy encompassed me. At times, we became so engrossed with her experiences that it became impossible to disengage ourselves emotionally. Now the frown of terror on her face and the agonized tone of her voice were almost too much to witness. I suddenly felt like shouting out in protest at what we were allowing this poor woman to relive.

Abruptly, in the midst of her groans, Betty slipped from a participant's role to that of an observer. As she relaxed, everyone breathed a sigh of relief.

Betty: I can feel them moving that thing around in my stomach or my body.... They've stopped. [*Very heavy breathing.*] And he's putting his hand on my head. [*Sigh, and heavy breathing.*] Now he's talking with them about something—something about something missing, missing...missing parts or something, I think he is saying.

Betty sometimes had difficulty interpreting the telepathic impressions the aliens generated, especially when they were not addressing her directly.

Betty: Oh! He's pushing that again...around, feeling things.... "I don't like this!"... Feels like he's going right around my stuff inside—feeling it, or something with that needle.... Oh-h-h, boy! He's stopped again and he's going over to them again.... They're looking at me—they're saying something about some kind of test.

Betty sobbed frantically and shouted at them: "I don't want any more tests! Get this thing out of me!"

Betty: He's coming over and he looks—he looks different. He is starting to take the thing out. Oh-h-h-h-h.... Ah-h-h-h.... [*Sigh*]

"Thank you." Betty thanked the alien for easing her pain by laying his hand on her head.

Betty: Oh-h-h. He's going back over, and he's talking with them about something.... They look a little bit concerned, as if they are trying to talk him into something. [*Shouts*] "I don't want any more tests!" He's coming over, and he told me I'll be all right. He is waving his hand over me. He said, "These things won't hurt you. Just lie very still—very still."

Later at the debriefing, we asked Betty about the entities' reaction to this part of the examination.

Ray: You said Quazgaa looked *different* when he took the needle out of your navel. How was he different?

Betty: He looked—uh, I don't know. His face didn't appear different, but it was something he sent off that appeared as if he was worried.

Fred: How did he look worried? What change did you see that told you that?

Betty: I didn't see it. I don't think I saw it in the facial features. It must have been a vibration or—a sensing something.

Fred: You mentioned also at one time that they looked a little bit concerned. That's sort of the same question.

Betty: But their faces didn't change. You could just somehow tell.

Fred: You're sensing it, that's what you're saying? You sensed it?

Betty: It must be that I'm sensing it.... It's not registering on their faces.

Fred: Okay, now, are you sensing more than Quazgaa? Are you sensing the others or only him?

Betty: No, only Quazgaa. The others wanted to run more tests.

Fred: No, but I'm saying, do you receive senses from *all* the beings?

Betty: Yes.

Fred: Can you separate which one you are getting the sense from?

Betty: No, I can't separate. They all look alike, except that Quazgaa is bigger. And I wouldn't be able to tell [distinguish] Quazgaa either if he wasn't among the others and a little taller.

Joseph: How did you know that the others wanted to run more tests?

Betty: Because they were speaking to him and—uh, he was objecting. I know he was objecting, and I know that they wanted to do some other things.

Joseph: You could *hear* a conversation between them? Or sense a communication between them?

Betty: I don't know. There was something there that I *knew*.

Joseph: You knew they were communicating, but you don't know how. You say they were talking to each other?

Betty: They were talking to each other. They were talking about the—what was being done, and what they wanted to do. And I don't know the tests that they wanted to do, but I knew they wanted to do other tests.

Joseph: Could you understand the thoughts they were *talking* to each other?

Betty: I may have, but I don't know right now.

She found it hard to explain how the aliens had communicated with her. It seemed as if she heard their voices in her mind.

Betty's eyes darted back and forth. She was puzzled. The entities were just standing there. Nothing seemed to be happening, and yet intuitively she felt that something *was* happening. Then her eyes caught a movement from above, and she stiffened. She saw some kind of mechanism emerge from the center of the domed ceiling and slowly descend toward her paralyzed body. (See Figure 23.)

Betty: ...Something up in the center of the ceiling—coming down! It's like a big *eye* of some kind.... I don't know, maybe like a lens. I don't know what it is.... And it's moving down, all the way down—by my stomach! And they are bringing it real close!

Betty was visibly panic-stricken.

Betty: I hope that thing doesn't hurt!... Oh, don't let it hurt.... [*Long pause*] It doesn't hurt, at least. [*Pause*] They are raising it up again.... And they are bringing it all the way up now.

Later, the debriefing questions turned to the lens-like device that had been lowered over her body.

Ray: This big *eye* that came down from the ceiling—was it attached to something?

Betty: I don't know. I couldn't see past that.

Ray: All you could see was just the thing coming down?

Betty: It was attached to the ceiling, yes.

Ray: What did it look like it was made of? Compare it with something that you're familiar with.

Betty: Plastic and glass.

Ray: What shape was it?

Betty: It was shaped like an eye—you know, an oval eye. But the round center piece was like a lens. I'll have to draw it. [See Figure 23 on page 72.]

"See?" Quazgaa said, after the lens retracted. "That didn't hurt, did it?"

"No, but the other things did."

"I'm very sorry," he answered. "It needed to be done."

"How much longer am I going to have to lie here?"

"Possibly a few more moments." Quazgaa assured her. "Just please relax."

Betty: And he waved his hand over me again.... He's going over, and they're looking at something over there. I can see—one, two, three, four of them. Their heads are looking down at something—must be studying something over there.

"Oh-h-h, how long am I going to have to stay here?" Betty groaned.

Quazgaa looked back at her and told her, "We will be just a moment."

After a few minutes, Quazgaa and his three smaller companions came over to the examining table and stood beside Betty. Quazgaa raised his hands.

Betty: And somehow, he's waving his hands over—my hands.

"When Quazgaa waved his hand over you," I later asked Betty, "how did you feel?"

Betty: He did this several times. I felt more relaxed. My hands feel better. And my legs and my feet—he's waving over those. And I'm sitting up all of a sudden, and...

Betty's mind was in turmoil. She still found it hard to believe that all of this was happening to her. Quite involuntarily, her body snapped to a sitting position and began to *float* above the table!

Betty: And I'm—like—being carried off there somehow, and carried, somehow? But nobody's touching me! It doesn't seem.... [*Sigh*] They are beside me, but seems like I'm being carried—carried over to the door.

When Betty's levitated body reached the wall where the door had been, she suddenly straightened out to a standing position between the entities.

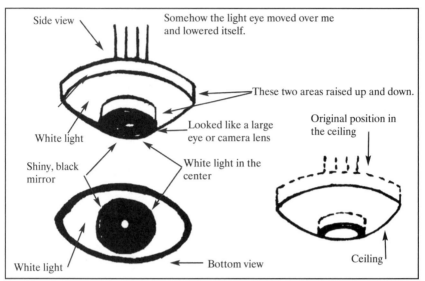

Figure 23: *The light over the examining table. June 19.*

Betty: And now I'm standing. One of them is in front of me again, and
             one in back of me. Looks like Quazgaa and two others. Three
             others [are] somewhere over to the side there. And the one in
             front of me is telling me to please follow him.

Betty left the examination area with two of the entities. Quazgaa and
several companions remained behind as the door flashed open and closed.

Betty: And we are going out the door, and we're in that same room. "What
             is that?" I can see something more now at that *hatch.* It comes out
             now, and there's like a honeycomb or something—I don't know what
             it is. I'm following them, and there's that place where I was under
             the light [i.e., the cleansing device]. They brought me back to that
             room where the pyramid thing points out.

Betty was returned to the dressing room.

Betty: And the door whooshes open. He gestures again for me to get
             dressed, and it's kind of dim in there. And I'm reaching down
             and picking up my clothes and my underthings—slipping my
             arms out and trying to get into my underthings. *"Oh, what is this
             all about, Jesus?"*

C·H·A·P·T·E·R 5

➤ Trip to an Alien Realm ≺

Betty hastily slipped into her own clothes. She felt secure in them. They provided a link with things familiar—home, family, and friends.

Betty: I'm getting dressed, and I put the garment down on the floor. And the garment seems to—sort of stick somehow to the stuff there...stick, although it didn't feel sticky on me, but it seems like it sticks there. I'm still trying to get dressed. I wonder what they are going to put me through next.

Betty finished dressing and shouted to her captors, "I'm ready! I'm ready!"

The door whooshed open and there they were. Again the two gnome-like beings asked her to follow them. Somehow she was automatically drawn between them, and they glided forward effortlessly. Betty found herself reentering the room where the elevator tube had terminated.

The trio glided toward a wall. A door flashed open and they entered an enclosed corridor that reminded Betty of a subway tunnel. It was at this point that she noticed they were floating above something like a track!

Betty: We are going through—like an underground corridor, all hollow— into another opening where it is light. And it's like a track we're going on, like a track. We are still walking, gliding—or something. My head feels so heavy. It feels so heavy. I can hardly hold it up.

We later asked Betty if she thought she had left the craft, because the area that she had been describing seemed too vast to have been within the UFO.

Betty: No, it doesn't seem as if I'm in the craft.

Joseph: How did you get out of the craft?

Betty: It was through that long black tunnel.

Ray: When you were going along this tunnel, were you walking with your feet?

Betty: No. We were just skimming on this black thing.

Ray: On it or above it?

Betty: Just a little above it. We were skimming on this black thing. I'm just following that other one and the other one is in back of me.

Ray: That black thing. You said it was like a track?

Betty: Yeah, it's like a track. It wasn't like we know a track.

Ray: How wide was it?

Betty: About as wide as your book, right there.

I glanced down at my hard-covered clipboard. It was only 9 inches wide.

Joseph: It wasn't any wider than that?

Betty: No, it was narrow.

Ray: Was it metal, or could you tell what it was made out of? Was it just one, or two, or three?

Betty: No. Again, to me—well, it was like...plastic maybe.

Jules: You must have been curious about where you were going. Did you ask them where you were going?

Betty: [*Softly*] I must have asked them.

Soon Betty saw light in front of her.

Betty: ...There is more light, and it is bright—now we're in there.

The three emerged into a curiously shaped compartment like a half cylinder or Quonset hut. Four glasslike chairs lined each side of the room. The escalator-like track ran between the peculiar chairs. (See Figure 24.)

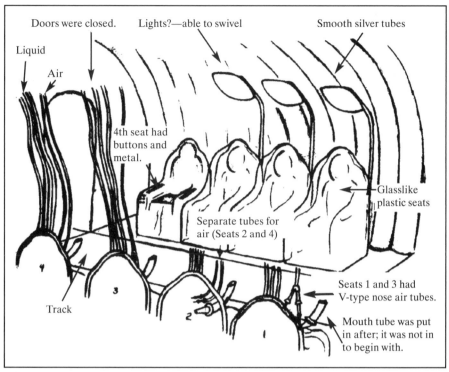

Figure 24: *The cylindrical room. June 19.*

Betty: And there are—there are some, like uh, glass?...uh...plastic?
Clear plastic seats on the side. And there are lights that come
up. And there's—one, and two, and three, and the fourth one
looks different. They're on two sides, and there's something in
the middle and it encloses somehow with glass. The glass things
are upward, or held up somehow.

The alien beings brought Betty to sit in one of the strange chairs. They
said, "Would you please be seated?"

"What is this going to do?" Betty asked.

"Please be seated," he said. "We will not harm you."

Betty felt somehow under their control. Their polite requests created
an illusion of free will, but in reality, she found that her choice always corresponded with their wishes. Her willpower seemed mesmerized by powerful influences beyond her ken. As she sat down, a transparent enclosure
came down around her. (See Figure 25 on page 76.)

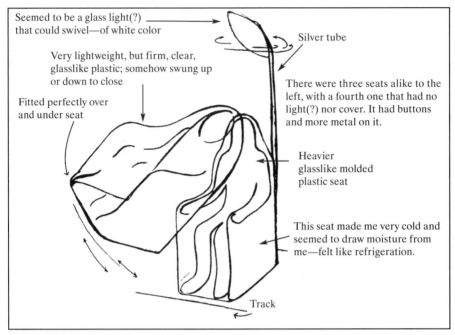

Figure 25: *The "cold" chair. June 19.*

Betty: I sat down in this thing and they put this glass around me, whatever—plastic? Clear plastic or clear glass.

"You said the chair was glass or plastic," Joseph Santangelo later asked her. "You sat in the chair. Did you touch it? Did you feel it with your hands?"

Betty: Yeah, I was sitting in it.

Joseph: There's a difference in feeling between glass and plastic.

Betty: I think it was plastic.

Now Betty became panicky.

Betty: I hope I can breathe in here! [*Pause*] There seems to be air. I feel so...[*Sigh*]...I feel I'm going to be knocked out from it. It feels like they are putting something cold in there. [*Sigh*] Oh! It feels like it is getting colder! [*Deep breathing*] It feels cold.

Her deep breaths continued. Betty's voice weakened to a whisper. "It feels very cold.... It feels like—feels like moisture is even being drawn from me.... And it's cold. The moisture is coming right out of me."

Her last sentence was extremely weak, as if she were enervated. The hypnotist reacted quickly.

Harold: You are only there as an *observer*. You are only there as an *observer*. You will now start to feel comfortable. You will feel very, very comfortable. Are you now feeling more and more comfortable?

Betty: Yes.

Harold: Are you?

Betty: A little.

Harold: Fine. Continue, please.

Betty: Uh [*weakly*], they have me in this thing. It's a glass thing. Clear plastic, or something. And [*sigh*] my legs feel funny from it.

Betty felt trapped, caged, and to those of us gathered around her in the office, the anxiety in her voice was distressing. Again, the hypnotist brought her relief.

Harold: Betty! I want you to relax for a few moments. Just relax. Make yourself very comfortable.

Her tense body relaxed and slumped back into the comfortable contours of the reclining chair. It was a convenient time to change recording tapes. After a few minutes, she was allowed to continue the bizarre escapade. Unfortunately, even stranger things awaited Betty and her listeners.

Harold: Please continue where you left off.

Betty: I'm in that glass thing—that encasing chair. I'm cold. And I've been in there a long time.... And the door [i.e., the covering] is starting to open. The other half of it is opening. And [*sigh*] the—uh, they've come for me again.

The entities beckoned to Betty, and in a sitting position, she *floated* to another of the odd-looking chairs.

Betty: And somehow the chamber is sort of weightless, because they just beckon me and I'm lifting up! I'm sort of in a sitting-down position, but I'm lifting up. And they're directing me over to the other side, where there are chairs similar to this. And I'm sitting down again.

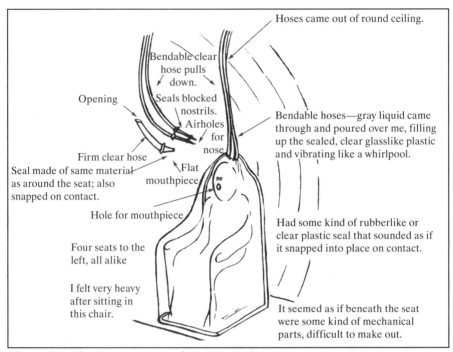

Hoses came out of round ceiling.

Bendable clear hose pulls down.

Opening

Seals blocked nostrils.

Airholes for nose

Firm clear hose

Seal made of same material as around the seat; also snapped on contact.

Flat mouthpiece

Hole for mouthpiece

Four seats to the left, all alike

I felt very heavy after sitting in this chair.

Bendable hoses—gray liquid came through and poured over me, filling up the sealed, clear glasslike plastic and vibrating like a whirlpool.

Had some kind of rubberlike or clear plastic seal that sounded as if it snapped into place on contact.

It seemed as if beneath the seat were some kind of mechanical parts, difficult to make out.

Figure 26: *The "immersion" chair. June 19.*

Terror filled Betty's heart when she was told that she was to be immersed in a liquid. The entities assured her that provision would be made to prevent her from drowning.

Betty: They're telling me that there are three tubes...that they are going to put liquid in here with me in it!

Betty became hysterical. "I'll drown if you do that!"

"No, you won't drown," they said. "We've provided something for you. It is a tube—three tubes. Just keep your eyes closed, and you will be fine."

A translucent canopy enshrouded Betty's body. Self-sealing tubes were connected to her mouth and nose. (See Figure 26.)

Betty: They are closing that and sealing it. And they've got a tube they are inserting into my mouth and two tubes for my nostrils. [*Softly*] Oh, my God! And that tube goes down, into my mouth, into my nostrils, and somehow it's sealed.

Later, I asked Betty if she could feel air coming down those tubes into her mouth or nostrils, or both.

Betty: Yeah, I could feel air coming out, yeah. Just as if I was living under water. You know, drawing air in and out.

Betty cringed as liquid of a grayish color flowed onto her head and down the sides of her cheeks. She closed her eyes and grimaced as the trickle became a constant flow of inrushing liquid.

Betty: They're letting some gray liquid pour down on my head and into that place. And it's—uh, I've got to remember to keep my eyes closed! He said to keep my eyes closed.

Betty softly repeated the telepathic instructions being sent from the alien creatures: "'Don't be afraid. Keep your eyes closed. Don't be afraid....' That liquid is filling up—and it's filling up fast.... Keep my eyes closed."

As the watery substance filled the chair-like enclosure, Betty felt soothing vibrations pulse rhythmically through her submerged body.

Betty: Oh-h-h-h, it's soothing—it's relaxing.... Oh-h-h-h, feels good.... Ah-h-h, feels good. Oh, it feels so good! It's like a whirlpool— vibrating around. And I can breathe all right, 'cause I'm breathing through my mouth and through my nose through those tubes.

The tranquilizing oscillations continued. The feeling of heaviness that had attended Betty from the onset of her experience dissipated. She became one with—in perfect resonance with—the undulating fluid. Suddenly, Betty started as a telepathic voice interrupted her reverie.

"'Yes?' They're calling me and telling me that they are going to give me something to drink, and for me to swallow it."

Now Betty became visibly upset.

"'What is it? What is it?'... They said not to be alarmed. It is something I must go through and take. 'What is it?'"

Betty waited expectantly. Soon, she felt a thick syrup seeping into her mouth through the connecting tube.

Betty: It is a—about a spoonful or so they are giving me through the tube, and it tastes sweet. Tastes good. Oh! This feels good! Oh, so relaxing. [*Sigh*] And it tastes...tasted good. It was sweet and thick, sort of like a cough syrup. And I'm just in here and that vibration is going around and around, and it feels good on me. I feel very relaxed—just like a whirlpool.

"Did they give you this water—syrup—through the tube?" Fred Youngren later asked her.

Betty: They gave it through the tube.

Betty felt as if she had been transported somewhere during her immersion in the enclosed chair. She later speculated that the strange tank-like apparatus somehow shielded her body from harmful effects while en route. Her intuition was well founded: It would appear that the strange craft *did* carry Betty somewhere. The events that followed indicated that it again landed and linked itself to the entrance of an alien realm.

Finally, the vibrations ceased. The gray fluid drained from the enclosure, and it opened again.

Betty: It's stopping—it's stopping now, and starting to drain. And I can't seem to open my eyes yet. I can feel it draining. And now the heaviness is coming back. My hands, and my arms, and my legs, and my feet feel heavy again.

Somehow, the entities had control of Betty's eye movement. They had taken safety precautions to assure that Betty would keep her eyelids closed during her immersion. Soon her eyes blinked open, and Betty was startled to see that each creature had a black hood over his head. (See Figure 27.)

Betty: They are coming in again. This time they've got something dark over their faces, both of them—two of them. "My head hurts."... They've got something dark over their faces like a—sort of like a *hood,* but not a point to it. It is just—over both of their faces.

"The black things that were over their heads," Joseph Santangelo reminded her. "Was it like a device that would allow them—a life support system? So they could survive?"

Betty: It didn't seem that way. It just seemed like a black hood over them—clothes, like a concealment.

One of the entities stepped forward and touched something on the chair.

Betty: The one in front leaned over a little and touched something on the seat there.... I don't know if it was a button or something.

Immediately Betty's hands and arms felt lighter.

Betty: I'm beginning to feel lighter in the hands and the arms. But my right leg and my feet are so heavy still.

"Follow us, please," they said. Betty struggled to get up out of the chair. Suddenly she again found some force pulling her between them.

I later asked if she was wet when she came out of this immersion chair.

Betty: Yes, I was.

Joseph: How did your clothes dry?

Betty: I don't know.

Joseph: They weren't clinging to you?

Betty: Yes, they were clinging.

In moments, the trio were again floating above the black track. Betty sighed unhappily. They were moving in the *opposite* direction from which they had entered the half-cylindrical room. As they reached the other end of the chamber, a door flashed open. It opened into a tunnel.

Betty: And we are—going through a tunnel. Looks like a dark tunnel. They have hoods over their heads. And it's a very dark tunnel.

During debriefing, Betty later described gliding along within the darkened tunnel: "Oh, it wasn't a huge, huge tunnel. It was about the height of this room, maybe even a little smaller." But the entities' dark hoods caused a frightening illusion.

Betty: Their suits look shiny, but because of that dark thing they have on, they look like they don't have any heads. Look—headless. [*Softly*] "I wanna go back!"

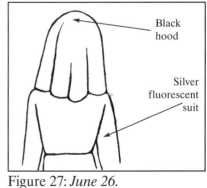

Figure 27: *June 26.*

"Can you describe those black hoods?" Jules Vaillancourt asked her later.

Betty: Just black. No shine to it. Just black cloth, because it blended right in with the tunnel so that all I saw was just the silver shining suits.

Jules: What was the source of illumination in the tunnel? You said it was really dark.

Betty: Their suits. The suits were the only illumination.

The aliens' silver suits glowed in the dark, barely illuminating their way. But the soft glow lighted the tunnel enough for Betty to see that it had been chipped out of stone.

Betty: I can see things that are chopped out. Oh, my head feels so heavy. I'm still going in that tunnel. I'm just going with them.

Later, Jules Vaillancourt prompted her.

Jules: Did it seem like a tube, like the inside of a garden hose, or did it seem chipped like a coal tunnel?

Betty: Chipped, like a coal tunnel.

At times they passed openings from intersecting tunnels.

Jules: How could you tell? It was so dark.

Betty: Because of their suits. The illumination came from those suits, and we would pass other tunnels, openings. I could tell that there were other tunnels there. As we would pass, I would see, like, a darker hole.

Jules: Did they seem... Of course, you wouldn't be able to tell how far the tunnels went in. As you went along, could you feel any temperature change?

Betty: No, it just was regular coolness, going through.

Jules: How fast was the speed? Could you see any traffic? Any signs of any other beings?

Betty: No.

Ray: You never touched the track? You were always above the track?

Betty: No, I couldn't touch anything with my hands or my legs and feet because they were too—uh, heavy, or something.

Betty wanted to go back, but found herself completely helpless.

Betty: Oh, my head feels heavy. [*Sigh*] And we're going, now we're going *upward* a little bit.

Abruptly, the track slanted upward. Ahead loomed a shiny, mirror-like obstruction.

Betty: And we are coming to some kind of a glass-mirror, or glass. [See Figure 28.]

She braced herself for a collision, which never occurred. The trio passed through the silvery material without encountering any assistance.

Betty: And they are going *through* it! We are going through it—through that mirror!

Betty squinted her eyes as they passed out of the tunnel into a place where the atmosphere was a *vibrating* red color. "The red looked like infrared light," she later explained. "It vibrated. It was like vibration through the air." The entities' silver suits reflected the shimmering color of this new environment.

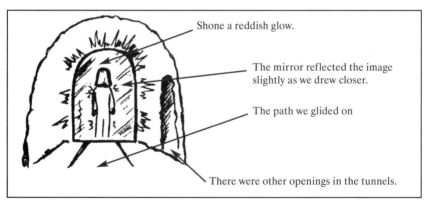

Figure 28: *The tunnel. June 26.*

Betty: I'm in a place where it's all red. The atmosphere is all red, vibrating red.... And their suits look red. Only their head-thing looks blackish red.

Later, during debriefing, Joseph Santangelo reminded her, "You said you saw red. Was that the horizon?"

Betty: That was after we came out of the dark tunnel. It was red all over.

Joseph: Below you? Above you? In front of you? Behind you?

Betty: Yeah, everything was red, except for the track that we were on. It was a dark color, like a black, but with the red hitting against it.

The black track stretched on ahead, between two square buildings with window-like openings.

Betty: We are going in this place, and there are buildings—square buildings with openings.

"Could you see the structure of the buildings?" Jules Vaillancourt later asked her. "Are they similar to ours?"

Betty: They seemed as if they're stucco or cement.

Joseph: Was it like a landscape, a—

Betty: In the red part, there wasn't. There wasn't any vegetable life.

Harold: Was there any foliage in the red portion?

Betty: Nothing.

Joseph: You were like in a red cloud?

Betty: No, it was—uh, there was land and there were buildings, but there was no vegetable life. Just land, and buildings....

Evidently, the scene was distant and none too distinct:

Betty: All you can do is make out the forms of things. And now we are passing—oh, boy, we are coming to where there's some beings!

Betty gaped in horror at what she saw crawling on the buildings. (See Figure 29.)

Betty: And these beings are—got two eyeballs...and there are loads of them. Oh, they're scary! And they've skinny arms and legs and kind of a full body. And their eyes can move every which way, and they can climb just like monkeys. They can climb up quickly and swiftly and down and around and in and out of windows. They are all over the place!

The weird creatures were headless. They had two large eyes located on the tips of stalks that emanated from the top of their bodies, and the stalks moved independently of each other.

Betty became very agitated as they passed by the frightful animals. "Who are these? Who are these?" she cried. The entities wouldn't tell her.

Figure 29: *The lemur or monkey-like creatures. June 19.*

Betty: But they are all around us, everywhere! They are all around and they keep looking at us.

"Was there animosity between the beings and these lemur [monkey] types?" Dr. Edelstein later asked her.

Betty: The beings just had the hoods over them.

The creatures' huge eyes gawked at Betty and her companions as they glided by. When they passed by without mishap, Betty breathed a sigh of relief.

"Was there anything else in the red place?" Dr. Edelstein later asked.

Betty: Just the buildings and those beings.

The track swept them forward.

Betty: We are in this red place. We are still going on this—I don't know if it's an escalator or what. It just seems like we are going along—further and further on...and we're coming to...

The threesome approached a circular membrane and passed through it without resistance into a place with a *green* atmosphere. (See Figure 30.)

Later, Joseph Santangelo asked her, "When did it change to green? I mean, did it change suddenly, or..."

Betty: No, we went a distance, and I seen those *things* [the monkey-like creatures]. And then it started to change.

The track curved upward. This new area was vast.

Betty: It's beautiful here. Oh, it's so beautiful here, and we are still along the thing. And now that we are in the green atmosphere, they are taking off those black hoods. And...going along and it seems like mist or sea or something off to the side there. Beautiful. And we're like on a narrow, narrow passage of land and we're gliding across it. And off to the side, I see—I don't know if they are fish or what. It looks like a combination fish and bird. And it seems like it's haze all over, and fog, and yet it's light so I can see it. And we are going someplace. I don't know where it is, up ahead, but it seems that we're going someplace.

Betty peered down upon strange plants, mist-enshrouded water, and a distant complex of buildings. The sheer vastness of this alien realm overwhelmed her senses. Where was she? What place was this? It reminded her of some legendary underground kingdom.

Betty: It's getting brighter green and beautiful. Oh, it's so beautiful. That one in front of me told me, "See, I told you not to be afraid." There's a lot of different stuff I'm seeing, but I can't describe it. It's just unusual and different. Plants are different. It's like, uh—long stems that come out in loops and the *different* colors. But they are green!

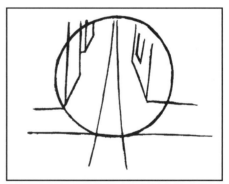

Figure 30: *The circular entrance between the red and green atmospheres. June 26.*

Betty sounded puzzled and frustrated at not being able to describe verbally what she saw.

Betty: I don't know how that can be, unless I'm just *feeling* or *thinking* the colors. Because it's green all around, and yet I can see the color in it. It's all green.... We are coming.... [*Pause*] Must be to a city or something, because there seems to be—buildings or something up ahead. It's just...[*pause*] I don't have the words to be able to explain it.

All of a sudden, Betty and her bracketing companions coasted to a halt. Other similar elevated tracks crisscrossed the area. They stopped to let something go by. Betty just watched, dumbfounded. Later she found nothing in her vocabulary to describe it.

Betty: We are stopping because there is something white there. There is something white. I don't know what it is! It is something like—I can't ever explain it. [*Sigh*]

"You mentioned starting and stopping," Fred Youngren reminded her later. "Could you feel yourself speed up and slow down? You know how in a car or train you can feel acceleration? Could you feel that?"

Betty: Yes.

Fred: Yes, but when you stopped, could you feel yourself being thrown forward? And when they started up, could you feel yourself being thrown backward?

Betty: No, there was no thrust. We just stopped—slowly stopped, and that was it. There was no—you know, fast stop.

Fred: Very smooth?

Betty: Yeah.

Their stop was brief, and soon they were on the move again. Betty was fascinated as she gazed down upon a building that reminded her of a pyramid. To its apex a sculptured head was affixed.

Betty: I'm seeing a pyramid. But this pyramid is a different kind of a pyramid—it has one big flat side and the others indent, sort of. We are going over it, high in the sky.

In a later debriefing, Jules Vaillancourt elicited from her a more complete description.

Jules: Getting back to those pyramids you mentioned—

Betty: *One* pyramid. With a white edge.

Jules: Where was the white edge? Was it on all three edges?

Betty: It was like a—okay, let's see if I can explain this. You take a star. You know, if you had a regular star, like this, right? Well, it had the edges, which were just like a star but it was cut off right in the middle, the center, so it was straight across. And then you just had the star.

Jules: You mean like a painted white edge or a source of illumination?

Betty: It was white, going down the whole edge.

Ray: Like if you took a knife and cut off the sharp edge and made it a flat edge all the way down and painted it white?

Betty: Yes, and then there was the head on the very top. There was no white there. It was just stopped at a certain section, and here was the big head on top—it still came to a point.

Ray: What was the head? Could you see?

Betty: It looked sort of like an Egyptian head, and it had like—you know, how they wear those hats? It was just a regular head. It wasn't fat like the Sphinx—the Sphinx has a big fat face. This had 11 cheeks, but it looked sort of feminine, yet male.

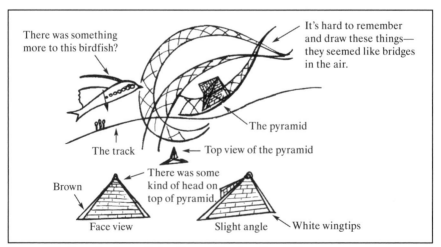

Figure 31: *Betty's view of the Green Realm. June 19.*

Jules: Do you think that you could draw a sketch of it now?

Betty: Not up close. I couldn't see the features that good. I could try. I'll attempt it, to get it down, but it was feminine-male. It was a combination of the two. [See Figure 31.]

I later asked Betty for some clarification on one point.

Ray: You say you were flying *over* this pyramid. What were you in? You said you were looking down. Have you been up in an airplane before? Was it like being up in an airplane?

Betty: It wasn't. No. That *thing* just went up into the air, and we just were going over it and able to look down.

Joseph: This *thing* that you were talking about. Was it like a bus?

Betty: No.... We're just standing up, that's all. It's just on this thing that we're standing on as we're going along.

Betty was talking about the same black track that transported them through the tunnel.

Joseph: And whatever that is, does it have any constraints? It just seems like you are out in the open, but that *track* is what is guiding you?

Betty: That's right.

Ray: Did you feel dizzy? Like you were going to fall off this thing at any time?

Betty: I felt dizzy a couple of times, yes, but I didn't feel as if I were going to fall off.

Jules: Were you breathing normally? I mean, you didn't have any kind of tubes or anything?

Betty: No, I was breathing normally.

Joseph: But you could see things below you as well as above you and to the side?

Betty: Yes, way below.

Ray: Did you see a horizon, like you were up in a...?

Betty: No, it was all fog and mist.

In her original description, of course, Betty had cited other buildings as well.

Betty: By that pyramid there's like a—I don't know if you would call them bridges or walkways, or what they are. And there's water there.

Jules Vaillancourt reminded Betty of this during debriefing.

Jules: Getting back to the city that you could see at a distance. Were you close enough to see any kind of beings? Any movement? How did you know it was a city?

Betty: It was definitely a city.

Jules: Were there high buildings?

Betty: There were, but they were so—they looked like, you know, a lot like science fiction. Big cities with all these different bridges all around....

Jules: Could you see activity?

Betty: No, I don't remember seeing activity. It was too far away. That was way over to the side there, way over to the side. The pyramid was closer than that. The city was way over to the side. There was a horizon because that was on the horizon and the sky was in back of it, the green sky.

Fred: Was there anything up in the sky? A sun?

Betty: No.

Harold: Was it artificially lit?

Betty: No.

Harold: Was there a dome?

Betty: Yes, there were domes.

Harold: Was there a large dome that contained this whole area that you were in?

Betty: No, there were many domes.

Ray: Where did you see these domes? Overhead?

Betty: No, off to the side. There were domes in the city.

Joseph: Betty, if you looked up, what was overhead?

Betty: Just endlessness of that green.

Betty's journey continued, however.

Betty: "Where are we going?" My head is so heavy. It feels funny. Still going up, and up—

Directly ahead of them, a bright light source came into view. It reflected off beautiful crystalline structures like giant prisms. Betty gazed in awe at the changing colors. The stark beauty of it all was frightening. (See Figure 32.)

Betty: And I'm coming before a bright light—crystals, bright, bright light, and clear crystals that have rainbows all in it. It is all crystal all around—all forms of crystal. I don't know what it is. I'm afraid! I want to go back! And the bright light up ahead. [*Sigh*] I want to go back. [*Sigh*] They are taking me through these crystals. That bright light is up ahead.... Oh-h-h-h-h, that bright light. We are stopping and the two are getting off the thing. And I'm just there, before the light.

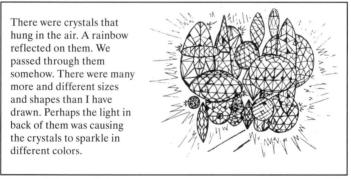

There were crystals that hung in the air. A rainbow reflected on them. We passed through them somehow. There were many more and different sizes and shapes than I have drawn. Perhaps the light in back of them was causing the crystals to sparkle in different colors.

Figure 32: *June 26.*

A vague form in front of the light slowly became more distinct. Astonished, Betty observed a huge bird standing directly in front of the dazzling light source. It was too big to be real, and yet it looked as if it were alive.

Betty: I'm seeing something like a large bird—huge, huge bird. It is standing with its wings and the light in back of it.

As they approached the birdlike apparition, the temperature became unbearably hot!

Betty: Whew! It is hot. I'm so hot. [*Panting*] I'm so hot. I feel like I'm burning, I'm so hot!

In the chair, Betty's body began to writhe in agony. The hypnotist immediately came to her rescue.

Harold: Just relax. I'm bringing you back to the present time, but this thought will remain in your mind where you have left off. And the next time that we conduct this, you will go to this state of mind.

Betty was allowed to recuperate. While she rested, we investigators hurriedly scanned our notes to frame questions for the debriefing period that began shortly thereafter.

Fred: Do you think that the ship was somehow connected to those places—through some other dimension, or something like that? I'm putting words in your mouth.

Betty: I think I went for a trip.

Fred: In the ship, do you think?

Betty: In the ship. I think I was kept in those glass chairs while we were going.

Fred: Okay, that's when you think the trip occurred?

Betty: Yes.

Fred: Do you think the glass chairs were in the ship?

Betty: Yes.

Fred: Okay, and that's when you think the voyage occurred. And then, when you reached the destination, you connected with this red and green place?

Betty: Yeah. When we reached the destination, we went through the black tunnel.

Fred: Still in the ship?

Betty: No, outside of the ship. There were...black tunnels.

Jules: Did they seem very long?

Betty: Yes, they seemed long.

Joseph: Did you have anything over you at that time? Your head felt heavy.

Betty: It felt like pressure or something on my head. My head was hurting and heavy from it, whatever it was. Even now, my head feels heavy from it.

Jules: Is this when the pear-head beings had the hoods on? And you didn't?

Betty: Yes, they had those black hoods. I didn't.

Joseph: Betty, when you said they put the—something dark over their heads—was that—do you think that was for protection?

Betty: I think so. That red, to me, that red seemed—they seemed worried about the red atmosphere. Because when they got into the green, they took those hoods off their heads.

Ray: What did they do with the hoods when they took them off?

Betty: We were out of the red atmosphere, and I don't know if they laid them to the side or if they kept them on their person.

Harold: Were these, ah, lemurs—were they on one side of the red atmosphere, or were they intermingled in the same area with the beings without the hoods?

Betty: No, they were just in one area.

Harold: There was nothing in the red place. The green place—was there foliage in the green place?

Betty: Yes. When we went into the green, there was vegetation. There was. I can't explain it.

I glanced at my watch. The debriefing period was about over. (Many of our debriefing questions and Betty's answers have, of course, been interpolated into the foregoing narrative.) Hastily we checked our notes for other questions that we had planned to ask Betty.

Ray: You seemed to be somehow attached to the track.... Do you think you left this earth and went to another world, or was this all someplace on this earth?

Betty: Not on top of this earth. I could have been inside the earth, but I went someplace else other than the earth.

Fred: You don't know whether it was another world then, or whether it was part of this earth?

Betty: Are you talking about another dimension?

Fred: No. I'm saying, did you leave this earth and go through space— to another planet? Or did this all happen on this earth?

Betty: I left this earth, yes, I left this earth. I believe we were in space, and somehow I believe we were in the center of the earth. Now how can you be in both?

Harold: It may be that this "other earth" that you went to, that the outside of it is like the shell, the housing. Everything that goes on, goes on within—like a large garage. The door opens and you can go in, and then you can leave it.

Our time was up, but many intended questions remained unanswered. We wondered about the strange bird, the dazzling light, and the heat that Betty had begun to describe in vivid terms. Could this have been real? Was she hallucinating? The answers would have to wait until the next session, scheduled for June 23, 1977.

Betty Ann Andreasson. Courtesy of Fred R. Youngren.

Becky Andreasson. Courtesy of Fred R. Youngren.

Dr. Harold J. Edelstein, who conducted the hypnosis sessions. Courtesy of Fred R. Youngren.

Back row (from left to right): David Stanton, Raymond E. Fowler, Virginia Neurath, Betty Andreasson.
Front row: Nancy McLaughlin, David Webb, Joseph Santangelo.

The investigative team. Courtesy of Fred R. Youngren.

Back row (from left to right): Deborah Vaillancourt, May Ellen Brady, Harold J. Edelstein, Becky Andreasson.
Front row: Jules Vaillancourt, Fred R. Youngren.

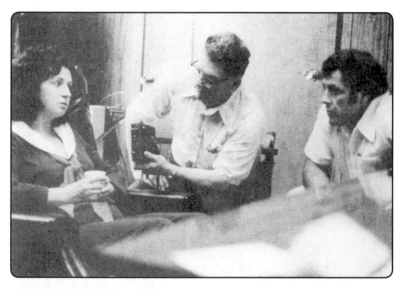

Joseph Santangelo and Jules Vaillancourt prepare to tape-record Betty's recollections under hypnosis. Courtesy of Fred R. Youngren.

Betty's face registers the fear and discomfort she experienced during the physical examination. Courtesy of Fred R. Youngren.

Still in hypnotic trance, Betty produces sketches of what she saw during her CE-IV experience. Courtesy of Fred R. Youngren.

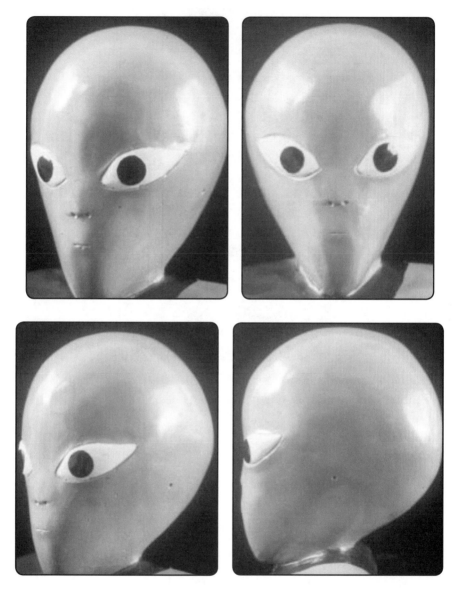

Based on Betty's sketches and recollections, Fred R. Youngren and his daughter Faith constructed this three-dimensional "mug shot" bust of Quazgaa, the apparent leader of the entities who abducted Betty. Courtesy of Fred R. Youngren.

The author, Raymond E. Fowler, with the Youngren model. Copyright Ralph Tourcotte, Beverly *[Massachusetts]* Times.

C•H•A•P•T•E•R 6

➤ A Vision of the Phoenix ➤

June 23 was a Thursday. Our next hypnotic regression session was scheduled for that evening. The summer sun still shone as investigators and witnesses filed into the offices of the New England Institute of Hypnosis. We were totally unprepared for what was about to take place. Betty was about to undergo the most painful and emotional segment of her total experience. Her suffering and ecstasy would be contagious. What we were about to witness would become etched indelibly on our minds, and in some hearts.

Betty lay back in the familiar chair. In a few minutes, she was in a deep trance. I sat at her feet, clipboard in hand, as Harold gave instructions to Betty.

Harold: Betty, I want you to take yourself back to just before we ended the session. Are you there? I want you to continue from that point on. Please do!

Betty: Just before we entered, or where we left off?

Harold: Do you need a little refreshing? To the incidents leading up to where we left off?

Betty: Where we left off? Where I was before that bird?

Harold: Okay, fine....

Betty began describing where she had left off at the last session. She started in the role of an observer, but quickly became an actual participant.

Betty: I'm standing before that large bird. It's very warm.... And that bird looks like an eagle to me. And it's living! It has a white head and there is light in back of it—real white light. Very, very big. And it has brown features.... And it's very, very hot here.... [*Heavy breathing*] The bird is just standing there, and it looks like it is holding back the light somehow. I'm just standing in front of it, and it's so hot. The bird, the feathers are just fluffed out. The light seems so bright in back of it. It's beautiful, bright light. [See Figure 33.]

Betty began to perspire and pant.

Betty: Oh, it's just standing there, and I see gold, gold specks flying around...like little tiny gold specks. Oh-h-h-h-h, it's hot! [*Blows her breath out*] The specks just keep on flying around, and that bird just keeps standing there. The light just keeps sending out rays. They keep on getting bigger and bigger. The rays keep on getting bigger and bigger. Oh, the heat is so strong! Oh-h, ow-w-w—makes me weak.

Betty cried out for help and writhed in agony.

Betty: Oh, Lord Jesus, I'm hot. Help me. Oh-h-h-h-h. [*Heavy breathing*] Oh-h-h-h. [*Begins to cry*] I'm so hot! Oh, oh, oh, oh-h-h-h!

At that point Betty began to scream in pain.

Betty: Take me out of it! Take me out of it! Take me out of it! Oh, oh, oh! [*Quick breaths*] Ah, ah, ah…I can't feel my hands! Oh, wow, wow, wow! Oh, my hands and my legs. My feet. Oh, oh. Oh, it feels like my hands are just vibrating so much and my feet are just vibrating like—oh, oh.

Suddenly Betty's body relaxed and she quieted down. It had all happened so fast that no one had time to react. We had become riveted to our seats with surprise.

Betty: Oh, I'm beginning to cool off a little. Ah, ah. Oh, my hands. Oh, my hands hurt.

Her voice took on a puzzled tone at that point.

Betty: There's a fire in front of me. A little fire, or something burning. I don't know what it is. It's just a little thing burning. My hands feel.... They hurt so much! They just keep on vibrating as if they feel like fire or something, as if I—oh, they hurt. [*Heavy breathing*]

I stood about this tall before it. It looked like a 15-foot eagle, but its neck was longer. It spread its wings, shielding the light behind it.

Figure 33: *The Great Bird. June 23.*

Betty's voice was filled with wonder. For her, the blinding light had dimmed. The seething temperature had dropped. Slowly she squinted her eyes open. The huge bird was nowhere to be seen. In its stead was a small fire. She watched it gradually dim to a reddish glow and then to a pile of gray ashes flecked with red embers. (See Figure 34 on page 104.)

Betty: That fire is burning down, and there are like coals there. I feel cold now. I feel cold.

Betty began to shiver all over.

Betty: Uh-h-h, oh-h-h, oh-h-h. I feel cold! [*Shivers*] Oh-h-h-h. [*Heavy breathing*] There's some kind of a glowing coal or something there. It was burning. It's just glowing right now. Oh-h-h. I feel some life returning to my hands. I feel better. That coal is just dying down to a reddish color. Oh-h.... It's getting gray, gray with red mixed with it.

Betty sounded astonished.

Betty: Now, looks like a *worm*, a big fat *worm*. It just looks like a big fat worm—a big fat gray worm just lying there.

The investigators cast incredulous looks at each other, wondering if we had pushed Betty too far. Then, seemingly from somewhere to her right (the entities were to her left), Betty heard what sounded like many voices blended into one booming voice!

Betty: I hear somebody speaking in a loud voice.

Then she hesitated and repeated what she heard.

Betty: "You have seen, and you have heard. Do you understand?" They called my name, and repeated it again in a louder voice. I said, "No, I don't understand what this is all about, why I'm even here." And they— whatever it was—said that "I have chosen you."

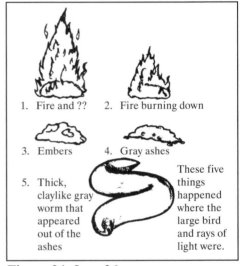

1. Fire and ??   2. Fire burning down

3. Embers   4. Gray ashes

5. Thick, claylike gray worm that appeared out of the ashes

These five things happened where the large bird and rays of light were.

Figure 34: *June 26.*

"For what have you chosen me?" Betty asked the voice.

"I have chosen you to show the world."

"Are you God?" Betty asked with wonder in her voice. "Are you the Lord God?"

"I shall show you as your time goes by" was the equivocal reply. Looks of puzzlement and concern passed among the investigators.

Harold rose from his chair and headed for an adjoining room, motioning me to follow him. I reluctantly left the room. Harold and I briefly consulted with each other about this weird turn of events. At this juncture, a religious connotation caused great consternation among us. It somehow seemed completely out of place. Meanwhile, in the office, Betty continued to converse with the voice.

Betty: "Are you my Lord Jesus? I would recognize my Lord Jesus." Oh, it says—"I love you. God is love, and I love you," they said or whatever it was. I say *they* but it seemed like one. [*Sigh*]

"Why was I brought here?" Betty asked again.

"Because I have chosen you."

"Why won't you tell me why and what for?"

"The time is not yet. It shall come. That which you have faith in, that which you trust."

Betty defensively proclaimed her Christian faith: "It is true. I have faith in God, and I have faith in Jesus Christ. Praise God, praise God, praise God. There is nothing that can harm me. There is nothing that can make me fear. I have faith in Jesus Christ!"

"We know, child," the voice answered. "We know, child, that you do. That is why you have been chosen. I am sending you back now. Fear not.... Be of comfort. Your own fear makes you feel these things. I would never harm you. It is your fear that you draw to your body, that causes you to feel these things. I can release you, but you must release yourself of that fear *through my son.*"

The words "through my son" suddenly became the catalyst for the most moving religious experience that I have ever witnessed. Betty's face literally shone with unrestrained joy as tears streamed down her beaming face.

Betty: Oh, praise God, praise God, praise God! [*Crying*] Thank you, Lord! [*Crying, sobbing*] I know, I know I am not worthy. Thank you for your Son. [*Uncontrollable sobbing*] Thank you for your Son.

Mere words—even actual transcriptions—cannot convey what Betty relived before us. To have both seen and heard Betty was a profound, unique experience, and listening to the tape recordings still provokes deep emotions to well up within me.

Betty continued to cry. We watched dumbfounded, perhaps a bit embarrassed. What was going to happen next? This otherworldly experience would leave Betty fearing for her sanity.

Later, the results of a psychiatric examination would set her mind at ease. But what was the stimulus for this bizarre event? Was it a compensatory dream triggered by Betty's religious beliefs and the effects of hypnosis? Had the aliens produced a physical or visionary object lesson for Betty's benefit?

Later, after Betty had finally concluded the reliving of her harrowing account, the investigators had many debriefing questions to ask her about this particular experience.

Ray: Would you explain again how you felt when you were standing before that bird?

Betty: When I was before the bird, I felt as if I were in the depths of weakness.

Jules: Was this bird alive?

Betty: The bird was alive. It was living. It was living.

Jules: How could you tell? Did it move?

Betty: You could see it breathing, and it was more living than anything I've ever seen living. I mean, we're living, right? But this was *really* living. The light in back of it was so living and alive.

Fred: Was there a sun or a moon or anything you could see in the sky?

Betty: Just that bright light that was in back of that huge bird with the fluffed-up feathers, and the rays just kept—reaching out further and further. And then finally there were specks of gold flying all over the place, and I was getting hotter.

Joseph: When you were standing in front of the bird where you said it was hot, was the moisture being drawn from your body, or was it like you were in an oven, or what?

Betty: That was terrible. I don't know what it was.

Joseph: Were your hands burning, or were you just hot?

Betty: It felt as if—I don't know what that feeling was. It's horrible. It felt as though something was permeating right through me. I don't know what it was. It was sort of the worst thing I've ever experienced.

Ray: What happened to the eagle? Did this just disappear and was replaced by fire?

Betty: I don't know what happened to the eagle because of what I was going through. The—whatever that was that was going through my body—it felt like something was piercing every cell in my body. You know how you can get a lump sum of pain? You know you can feel pain in the whole body? This was like it had pierced every cell or every portion of my body.

Though truly incredible, Betty's account up to this point had nonetheless roughly paralleled other reported CE-IVs. The bird episode, however, does not fit. Yet for Betty, her bittersweet rendezvous with the bird was just as real as every other facet of her story.

Ray: Do you have the impression that this bird thing was just as real as all the events leading up to it?

Betty: It is more real.

Ray: It wasn't like going into a dream state and having a dream of symbols, and so forth?

Betty: No, I could believe that the red atmosphere and the green atmosphere could be a dream state, but never the bird and the light and what I experienced. That part! I never want to have to go back to that part!

J. Allen Hynek has said that reports of Close Encounters of the Third Kind (now named Close Encounters of the Fourth Kind) are characterized by a high degree of *strangeness*. Indeed, this bizarre segment is essential to the unity of the overall narrative. We dare not dismiss it, because it may provide the focal point, the very reason, for the abduction of Betty Andreasson.

Fred: You told us about hearing a loud voice that talked with you.

Joseph: Could you see where the voice came from?

Betty: No, it came from the side.

Fred: Can you describe that location?

Betty: That was off to the right. It seemed off to the right. I couldn't see anything.

Fred: Were you on this elevated pathway?

Betty: No, I was standing right in front of where that burning fire had taken place.

Fred: You had come down to the ground?

Betty: There was a—uh, like a foundation. Just enough foundation for that path. That's when it went onto the ground. Yes, the sea was off to the side, and there was mist, and then it had that narrow land and it did finally go onto some kind of surface and was going up.

Jules: What color was the sea?

Betty: It seemed very dark, but it was green—very, very dark. It was choppy. After it had cleared, it looked smooth, sort of smooth glass.

Ray: You could see the shoreline?

Betty: No, it went off into mist.

Joseph: But it was clear? A loud, clear voice to you?

Betty: Yes, it was a loud, clear voice.

Ray: It told you, "You've seen this. Do you understand?" You said, "No." Do you understand what this was all about?

Betty: I understand now that I went through an initiation of some kind.

Joseph: Do you know why you were crying?

Betty: It was from love.

Jules: The tears. They seemed like elation—happy tears.

Betty: It was that. I really believe it was God that spoke to me. I feel funny about saying it because—I mean, God has made all things, and is even present in everything. And yet, here I was standing and He spoke to me. And I know it was through His Son, you know, that, uh—and I just felt the love of Jesus.

Virginia: (sitting in on the session) Do you identify the radiation, the voice, with God?

Betty: I don't feel as if that bird was God. I feel as if the light in back of the bird was the radiation of God. I could not see God. All I did was hear the voice, and that was it. I could not see any form, and I don't think I even wanted to look upon the form, if there was such a form.

Ray: The impression I got is that right up until that time, you still had doubts regarding that this was really God. Right up to that time, you still had doubts why this was happening to you, and you wanted an answer. When he referred to his Son, it seemed that all of a sudden you realized what this was all about, and that's when you started to have this experience. It was almost like a dam burst, you know. You had been holding all this back, and all of a sudden you realized somehow or other that this was of God, and that is when you started to have this ecstatic experience.

Betty: I believe it *is* of God. But I still feel, who's going to believe me? I mean, I trust all of you and everything, but there is doubt in my mind that even you really believe me about an experience such as that, because it is unbelievable.

Could Betty's encounter with the huge bird best be described as an intense *religious* experience? One is tempted to propose that the stimulus for the event was Betty's strong religious background. This is quite possible, of course, and already we have some basis for such a suggestion.

Earlier we saw that Betty's Christian beliefs provided a desperately needed rationale when the alien beings passed through a closed door into her kitchen. "I'm thinking they must be angels," Betty had said, "and scriptures keep coming into my mind." Again, when the entities asked Betty for "knowledge tried by fire," she showed them a Bible. When Quazgaa somehow produced four little books with blank, luminous pages, Betty automatically assumed that he had reproduced her Bible.

Throughout the abduction experience, Betty prayed within the context of her Christian faith, the very warp and woof of her life. Therefore, is it not possible that Betty's subliminal mind sought for theological meaning to an otherwise meaningless, terrifying, and painful experience? The very concepts of UFOs and extraterrestrial life had no place within the confines of fundamentalist Christianity. Perhaps, heightened by the effects of hypnosis, Betty's subconscious mind accommodated and reinterpreted the troubling elements of her UFO encounter. The result? A vivid, relived compensatory dream.

This hypothesis might seem quite logical and appropriate at first thought, but it has a serious flaw. The experience, whether dream or reality, did not concern itself with some readily discernible aspect or symbol of *modern* Christianity. Quite the contrary.

Ray: As far as you're concerned, there was no symbolic message or meaning behind these—things?

Betty: Well, my sister and I were talking…. She had thought that she had seen that symbol someplace before, with the wings down. Some kind of Inca thing, Indian.

Ray: The symbol for the United States is a bald eagle.

Betty: But this had its wings down like this and my sister said, "That looks like a symbol that the Incas used, or Indians in times past."

Ray: On their uniforms they had what looked like a bird.

Betty: That's right! [See Figure 5 on page 34.]

Ray: Was it the same type of thing?

Betty: Yes, it was. It was the same type of thing. That's right!

Ray: We have various symbols. We have the American flag flying everywhere…. I was thinking that maybe this symbol represented something for them. They thought that you would understand this, and then they seemed to explain it to you in a sense. They seemed to give you some kind of a message afterward—I was wondering if that was directly related to what you saw.

Betty: Well, another thing—as I said, my sister Shirley looked up about the Phoenix bird….

Indeed, upon investigation, we found that Betty seems to have witnessed the death and rebirth of the legendary Phoenix. *Collier Encyclopedia* describes a bird almost identical to what Betty reported:

Phoenix, a legendary bird that builds its own funeral pyre and is reborn from its own ashes. Sacred in ancient Egypt, the Phoenix, which was always male and had a beautiful red and gold plumage, was fabled to live for 500 years or longer. At the end of that time, it built a nest from twigs of spice trees, to which it set fire. *Both the bird and its nest were consumed in the flames. Out of the ashes, a worm emerged,* from which the new Phoenix grew.[1] [emphasis added]

It is interesting to note that the legendary Phoenix made its nest from "twigs of spice trees."

Ray: Did you feel any air or smell anything at all during this whole thing? Did you smell anything?

Betty: I might have smelled something when that was burning.

Ray: What was burning? The eagle?

Betty: When that thing was burning. Sort of like a sweet incense smell when those ashes were burning—or whatever that thing was that was burning.

Smoldering spice-twig ashes would probably give off a smell like incense! Interestingly enough, *Collier Encyclopedia* adds that "The Phoenix figures prominently in *early Christian* art and literature as a symbol of immortality and the resurrection."[2] [emphasis added]

Her confrontation with a mythical monster was unsettling, to say the least. Was there a relationship between the phoenix and the insignia of a bird on the aliens' uniforms? Exactly who or what was the *voice*? These and many other questions would occupy our minds for months during our lengthy analysis and evaluation of the Andreasson Affair. However, Betty's experience did not end with the bird. There was much more to come.

C·H·A·P·T·E·R 7

➤ The Return ➤

Betty's sobbing gradually ceased. From the expression on her face, it was obvious that her fiery ordeal was now over and something else was about to occur.

Betty: Somehow, I'm being turned around. Oh, and that feeling is in my hands. "Oh, help me not to fear!" My hands feel—my legs and my feet. I'm going back on that thing [the track], and, ah, I'm stopping. And those angels—I guess—one is getting in front of me, and one is in back of me. And we are going along, and we are going through those crystals again. And the crystals aren't quite as shiny and like a rainbow as before.

We listened intently as Betty and the two entities retraced their original path via the black track. Betty began speculating out loud concerning the heaviness that she felt in her legs. It seemed as if the force that kept Betty glued to a position just above the track was also responsible for her severe physical discomfort.

Betty: I think maybe why my feet are like that—I must be, uh, glued to that thing, because there are no railings and there's nothing holding me in. And I'm just gliding along that thing, and it's not very wide. Maybe it's so I won't fall off or something or other. Oh, my legs feel so heavy. And we are just gliding along on that thing. And we're way up in the air. And that green and blue-colored atmosphere, it's just beautiful. Somehow, I just don't want even to leave. It's just so beautiful.

In a later debriefing, we tried to recover Betty's impressions of this odd landscape on this, her "second time around."

Fred: When you were in the green place, was there a sky?

Betty: The green atmosphere was the sky, and then it was also blue. It was green—beautiful green—and it was also blue.

Ray: Was there a separation between the green and the blue?

Betty: No, the green and blue were mixed. It was bright, bright green—emerald green—and then it was like blue.

Fred: Were there shadows? In other words, I'm looking for a light source. Was there a light source?

Betty: I don't remember any shadows. The only thing that I remember is going in through the crystals. It was bright, and there was a rainbow all around, but going out it was not as bright, and the rainbow was much dimmer.

Fred: Was there a horizon?

Betty: Yes, there was. There was like a top, but it's funny because—ah, what we were traveling on had no girders or anything. It was just in the air.

Fred: Suspended?

Betty: Yeah.

Fred: Did you feel weightless at that point?

Betty: My legs felt heavy, my hands felt heavy. The rest of me just felt regular, I guess.

The hypnotic impression of the landscape matched her previous description:

Betty: And, uh, we are just going along on that thing. I see water all around, and it's not as choppy as it was before. Oh, my legs feel just like bricks. Why? My hands and my legs, they just feel like they're stone. Ah, but it's like a sea, a clear calm sea. Oh, my legs! And, uh, we are just going *down*. And I see mist to the side. And we keep on going. Seems like a long way, and I'm coming to—uh, there's that pyramid again. Ah, it has that white on the edges. And that head and those bridges, or something or other. I don't know.

Later, during debriefing, Betty elaborated.

Betty: There was—uh, there was water that was very choppy when I was going, like a big sea. There was land, but it was, if you call it a horizon, it was like there was mist all around, but yet it did go into the green. The green blended into the green, and yet at times I was seeing the colors of the plants. I saw the color of the—the fish, bird fish. I saw the color of the pyramid, and yet it was green.

Again she obtained a brief glimpse of the city-like structure off in the distance.

Betty: Off to the side there is some kind of—something like a city or something. I don't know what it is. It is too different than I've ever seen before. I just can't explain it. It's beautiful. Oh, my feet and my legs! I'm just going along and the atmosphere is getting green, all over the place—green.

As they came closer to the entrance to the red area, the transportation track continued to dip downward. Again, they approached the partition that divides the green and red realms.

Betty: We are coming up to something that is [*Sigh*]—a veil? Or something. Not a veil, but a division of color or something or other, 'cause we are coming to that red stuff again. We are just going down. We are going into that red atmosphere. It seems somehow there is a *circle* there. It is divided from green and the red—and it's, uh, like I've been in solidity. And all of a sudden I'm going into another solidity of red. And, uh, it doesn't feel solid, but it is solid. And it's red—very, very pulsating—like red. It's the same place.

Betty found it hard to describe the green and red atmosphere. As she later recalled while out of trance, each was so dense and prominent that they appeared like two solids separated by a circular membrane.

Fred: Okay, I'm interested in the *red place* you went. Where do you think that was? Do you have any thoughts? Can you tell us anything about that?

Betty: No, I think it's a place. I think it's a place, a particular place.

Fred: Was there a sky there? Could you see a sky?

Betty: Just the red atmosphere. It was solid, and yet it had air like this. It was like—I don't know how to explain this, but it was solid.

Fred: Same color red everywhere?

Betty: Yes, same color—no, no, I mean, how can I explain that? I don't know how to explain.

Fred: What do you mean by solid? Like moving through water? Were you like under the water, and it was red water with light everywhere, and you were moving through that? Or was it like moving through a solid material?

Betty: It was a solid, but it was—

Fred: Like moving through the earth? Is that what you mean? Like you were going through ground?

Betty: I felt just like I am right now. I felt the air moved about me, but I knew it was solid. It was like a—

Fred: You were in a vehicle?

Betty: No, I was just standing on that thing there, just gliding. It was just a track that you just stood on, and it felt like my feet were just glued to it. It felt heavy from my knees down—like two stones were there. I felt pricking, a constant pricking like pins and needles.

Fred: And you were moving through something solid?

Betty: I was going through something solid, but it seemed just like this.

Ray: When did you think it was solid?

Betty: When I came back. Not until I came back.

Ray: This is the impression that I got: you didn't really talk about this "solid" bit until you realized that the green and the red had some kind of veil between them, and there was no mixture. It's as though there was something invisible that was keeping the red out of the green.

Betty: That's right. If you took—okay, if you had a square solid block of red glass and then you had a green one, and you just put the two together. That's what it was like.

Ray: Suppose you took a solid block of clear glass and you had an— I'll say an invisible force field, for want of a better term. And then, you put red gas in the left and green gas in the right, and you somehow could pass through that force field. Is that what you mean by solid—that they couldn't mix?

Betty: That's right, they couldn't mix. But I don't know.

Ray: Is that why you called it solid? Because they couldn't mix?

Betty: Yes, they couldn't mix. There was a *circle* that allowed us to go through it—from the green into the red. And then from the red into that tunnel. Going back, I saw a corridor, and it just kept on whirling and whirling and whirling. We were going through it, but it had no sides.

Back in the "red zone," they again passed between the square buildings with their grotesque occupants. Betty shuddered as they glided by the little stalk-eyed creatures.

Betty: They just bug their eyes out at me, and they crawl up and down those walls, in and out those windows. They are just there—all over the place. Big bug-eyed. And they can move their eyes any old place. Oh, I'm tired.

Later, I asked, "Did you *hear* anything, other than the voices in your mind? Did you ever hear any sound when you were going over the track— from the city, from the strange beings with the eyes?" Betty's answer was a simple no.

Then Betty saw another circular orifice dead ahead of them. She recognized it as the entrance to the tunnel.

Betty: And we are still going through that red atmosphere. We're coming up to that *circle* again. And it's like a mirror. We're going to go through something like a mirror. I guess it's that same mirror. Somehow it's whirling, whirling, uh—what is it? A whirling circle somehow that is, like drawing us into that whirling circle, through that mirror. It's just whirling—keeps on whirling. And we're breaking through that mirror now. Doesn't hurt, but we're going through it!

In an instant, they were plunged into darkness. Once again, Betty glided along within the confines of the dark rock-hewn tunnel.

Betty: And we are in that black...[*Pause*] blackness now. And we're just going along on that black walk, whatever it is. Can't see anything anyway, just their silver suits. I don't even see their heads, just the silver suit in front of me.

At this juncture, Harold interrupted Betty so that we could change the recording tapes.

Harold: Betty, just relax, just make yourself as comfortable as you possibly can be. Just refresh yourself—let me just make you a little bit more comfortable.

After the tapes were changed, Harold prepared Betty for questioning: "Betty, you are following someone, and all you could see was the silver cape. Will you please continue?"

Betty quickly corrected him.

Betty: It was not a silver *cape* that I was following. It was a silver *suit*!

Harold: Oh, a silver *suit!* I'm sorry; continue.

Betty: It was a silver—silver suit. And we are going along in this dark tunnel and, uh, we're just gliding along. And just keep on going and going and going, it seems like. We are in there a long time, it feels like.

Finally Betty glimpsed a shaft of light far up ahead. As they came closer, she was surprised to see a transparent door to the half-cylinder room. It had not been transparent before, when she had exited through it from the other side.

Betty: And we are coming now to some light. And I see those glass seats again up ahead. Oh, that door, that end part is not silver—it's, uh, glass, 'cause I can see through. It's like a glass, whatever it is—much glass. And we're getting closer to it, and the door is going up!

The three entered the room, and Betty watched curiously as the two little men took off their black hoods.

Betty: We're inside that room, and they're stopping and they're getting off the thing. We're stopped, and they're removing those things—their hoods—and putting them down someplace. One's putting them on one side, and the other's on the other side.

Betty was somehow floated onto one of the strange glass chairs. It was different from the other chairs, in that it had inlaid metal strips on its arms and on its seat.

Betty: We're right next to—oh no, they're setting me down in that strange seat there. That different one from all the others, with those buttons and those steel things there. I'm sitting down in it.... And they're putting my hands—oh.... [*Sigh*] They put my hands and arms on that thing.... And they're looking at me with their eyes somehow, for some reason, and—ah, oh-h-h-h-h!

Betty's body jumped violently—once, twice! The dual convulsions startled us. During a later debriefing, we asked her what had occurred.

Jules: At the last session, your body actually jolted twice. What was happening then?

Betty: When he touched that button. I don't know what the purpose was.

On the fourth chair was something that looked like a button. One of the entities touched it twice. Simultaneously, Betty had felt twin electrical shocks course through her body.

Ray: Notice on the drawing of the chair. [See Figure 24 on page 75.] You had buttons over here. The bars are here. Where were your arms in relation to the bars?

Betty: I was on them, like that.

Ray: Did the jolt come from the bars?

Betty: The bars were metal, and they pressed down.

Ray: So this was the metal part here?

Betty: It was metal here [*points to arms of seat*] and a metal seat [*points to sitting area*].

Ray: Okay, guess I didn't know that.

Jules: Where was the glass?

Betty: The glass was molded—or plastic, whatever it was—just like the other ones.

Ray: It was covered with metal. In other words, the metal would be embedded?

Betty: Yeah.

For a moment, during the original hypnosis session, I had thought that the entranced Betty had experienced a heart seizure. I breathed a bit easier when she began to speak again.

Betty: [*Heavy breathing*] I hear a whirring sound...and he's opening up one of my eyes.

"When they put you on the chair with the buttons and the metal," I told her later, "you were describing what had happened up to that point as if you could see it all. When you were jolted, you mentioned that you opened your eyes—which would indicate that you had closed your eyes at some point prior to that. When did you close your eyes? How could you describe all this with your eyes closed?"

Betty: When I was on the seat, I did not have my eyes open. Then there were two jolts and they—opened my right eye, as my eyes were not open.

Ray: Okay, so we know your eyes were closed when you sat down in that special chair with the buttons. Do you remember when they closed your eyes?

Betty: Somehow they were closed. I don't know, because I saw him go over and touch something on the wall. I saw him touch the buttons. After—I think after, or during the jolt—in between the two jolts, I think my eyes must have been closed because he came over and he opened my right eye. When I was in the first seat, I felt like I was being frozen. I felt frozen and becoming very heavy, like water was just—moisture was just being drawn from me somehow.

Jules: Another thing—when you were in the capsule, did you notice anyone else in the seats?

Betty: No, there was no one else there.

Jules: You were the only one? All the other seats were vacant?

Betty: Uh-huh.

Fred: When you were in this vehicle that had the seats in it, could you sense that it moved? Could you tell whether you were going up or down?

Betty: No, I couldn't tell up or down. It seemed like there was a whirling going on, somehow a whirling, but yet the room wasn't whirling.

Fred: Did you feel like you were being pressed down in the seat—or did you feel like you were floating?

Betty: When I got out of the seat, I felt floating....

Indeed, Betty was removed from her "cold seat" by something that seems to have been an automatic levitation device.

Betty: [*Heavy sighs*] He's shaking his head or something, and—standing there.... And they are touching something on the wall over there by the door. I'm just floating off that seat! I'm just floating down to *that chair* again. Oh, my feet and my hands feel so heavy!

Betty found herself seated in the immersion chair, and again subjected to its calming effects.

Betty: They're snapping that seat in place. They are putting those things in my nose and my mouth.

The liquid again poured in around her. She experienced the same soothing vibrations.

Betty: Oh, that feels good. [*Sigh*] That feels real good. They're putting, ah, that stuff all in it. It's getting, uh—and I'm breathing through the tube. It feels good, and they're putting that, like a whirlpool on. [*Whispers*] Oh, this is so good!

The entities called to Betty, again warning her that a liquid would flow into her mouth through the connecting tube. She was told to swallow.

Betty: "What?" Okay.... They gave me some more of that—um, syrup. Mmmm, it tastes good and wakes me up like—very sweet. I can still taste that taste. Feels good and smooth. It's sweet, like a syrup, but it doesn't make me feel sick, 'cause usually syrups make me feel sick if I have too thick a syrup on pancakes or something.

Betty became totally absorbed with the pleasant feelings that pulsated through her body, but she was jolted back to reality by a persistent tapping sound.

Betty: They're tapping on that glass thing for some reason. And they are saying, "Betty, are you comfortable?" "Yes, I like it in here." They said they are going to let me stay a few more moments.... Oh, feels good.

She later commented that this was one of the few times they had displayed overt concern for her welfare.

Betty: They had kindness within them. They had obedience within them. They—uh, it was only a few occasions that I saw sensitivity in them—when I called out to Jesus, when I was getting changed—and, ah, also when I was in that seat where the liquid was coming in, they—seemed as if there was something special.

Virginia: They treated you with a sort of—

Betty: A lot more sympathy. On the way back, they were much more sensitive than the way going.

Virginia: By sensitivity, you mean...?

Betty: Sympathetic toward my feelings.

Soon Betty felt the level of the fluid lower around her immersed body.

Betty: Here it goes. They're beginning to drain it. I can feel it going down. It feels funny when it drains. I can feel it at the top of my head—as it drains and releases, I can feel it just being lower and lower. Like a thick, thick thing—like an oil or something. Feels like my—whenever I have an oil bath, like I'm being coated by oil or something.... When I let the water out, and there's a film of oil on top of it as it drains down.

Betty watched the entities remove the tubes connected to her mouth and nostrils.

Betty: Ah, it's down to about my waist now, and they're removing the mouthpiece, and the nose pieces.... It's down to the bottom because I can hear it unsnap and raise up. [*Sigh*] That was good. And they're just busy putting the stuff away, I guess—or doing something, raising it up with something or other. Goes up automatically, but just the hoses they have to put away.

By this time, Betty was quite sure she knew which chair they would put her in next. However, they put her in a different one.

Betty: I'm just floating up. I'm going over to the chair in front of me. Wait a minute, I'm not going over to the front. They're putting me in the *first* one instead—and they're closing it down.

This chair, too, had a transparent enclosure that was lowered over Betty's seated body.

Betty: And, ah, I'm just sitting there. And there's warmness there. I feel nice and warm. There's air coming in it, but this time I feel warm, not cold. It is very warm and [*Sigh*] I'm just sitting there and relaxing in the warmth of it. And there's air coming in it. I can hear the air this time, and, it's warm, very warm. I feel very comfortable— very comfortable there. I can feel the warm air blowing against me.

"On the way back," Jules Vaillancourt later reminded her, "you sat in a different seat. Can you describe getting in the seat and the fact that the temperature change was different?"

Betty: That was on the *other side* of that round cylinder thing.... I thought they started floating me toward the very same place... where I was frozen—but I went over to the first seat and—

Jules: Why do you say frozen?

Betty: Because I think that is what happened.

Jules: You said it felt good.

Betty: No, that's the first time. The second time, coming back, it was the warm air coming in that made me feel good. Maybe they were drying me off. I don't know—I was wet from that gray liquid.

The enclosure opened automatically, and Betty felt the chair swinging upward. A fixture swiveled over her.

Betty: It's stopping now and the chair is swinging up automatically. And whatever that thing is up there, it's swiveled over, and is over me. And it's a bright purplish-color pink light shining down on me. Oh [*Sigh*], just a light. And out of that light is little tiny streaks again, like I saw when I was in that other place [the cleansing device]. It's a purple light, purple-pink, with streaks in that purple-pink light, and it's shining down on me. [See Figure 35.]

Betty's conscious recall was slightly more precise.

Betty: After the seat went up, the swivel thing came over, and it changed form. It came down like this, and it had a gray, dark gray—almost a sort of black—glass on it, on the edges.... Then this purple light was coming down. Just like that bug catcher for insects, that purple light that comes down. As it came down further, it became pink and there were streaks, just light streaks, that just kept darting out of it—you know, from the whole thing. Just like the cleansing light, it had the same light streaks as that.

Betty watched as the other entity seemed to be reaching for something.

Betty: He's finishing up something. Oh, and he's grabbing a ball of—a white ball. There are two white balls there. I didn't see them before, but he's grabbing them. He's got two balls in his hand, one bigger than the other.

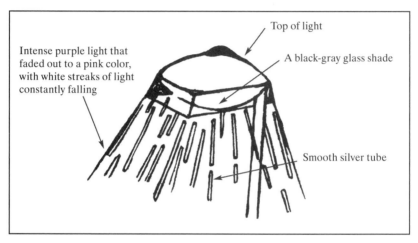

Figure 35: *The swivel light in the cylindrical room. June 26.*

The other entity had taken the white glowing spheres from two cylindrical pedestals. He carried one in each hand as he took up the familiar position directly behind Betty.

Betty: And he's in back of us now, 'cause we're moving on. That door goes whooshing up. We're just moving on—I just keep on moving, through that same place, I guess, where we were before 'cause I think I see like that elevator we were on before—that tube, whatever it was.

Betty recognized the elevator tube through which she had floated down from the upper room shortly after she had been taken aboard the UFO. (See Figure 36 on page 126.)

Betty: And then we're up to that door, and we're—it's whooshing open!... And we're back in that room. I see the hatch there.

And on the floor—on the floor it's up, and it's got a huge spring underneath it. A huge spring with four other springs.

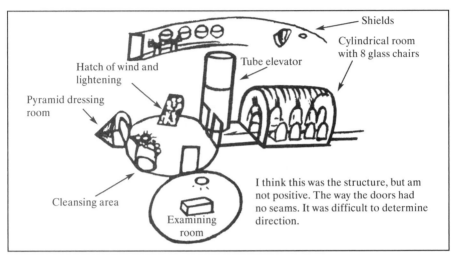

Figure 36: *Betty's conjectural layout of the craft. June 19.*

This hatch, or rectangular enclosure, had previously protruded downward out of the wall into the floor. Now it had been telescoped into the wall, revealing what appeared to be an opening in the floor.

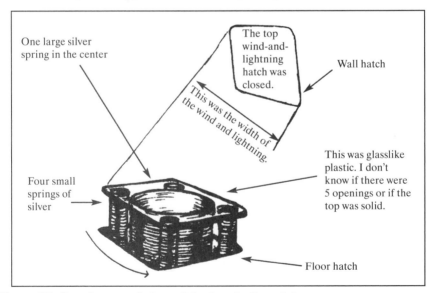

Figure 37: *Betty's second view of the hatch. June 26.*

"These huge springs you mentioned," Jules Vaillancourt later said during debriefing, "do you think you could get that on paper?"

Betty: Yeah, I'll try and get those. They were a silver-white.

Jules: Like a coil type of spring?

Betty: A coil-type of spring, silver-white—like aluminum. [See Figure 37 on page 126.]

The trio had glided to a halt. Betty glanced around her. Nothing seemed to be happening.

Betty: We're just standing there. I don't know why. "What are we waiting for!" They said Quazgaa would like to speak to me....

C·H·AP·T·E·R 8

≻ Quazgaa's Farewell ≺

Betty and her two alien companions stood silently waiting. Thoughts of home and family briefly surfaced, then slipped away. The aura of friendliness emanating from her captors caused Betty to remain relatively calm. Only the most trying circumstances had caused her emotions to override their strange, hypnotic-like influence over her. At such times, a waving or laying on of hands by the aliens restored her calmness and eased discomfort. Now a door flashed open, and Quazgaa entered the room.

Betty: We're just standing and waiting and that door opens! And Quazgaa's in that silver suit. He comes over to me.

The little man looked up at Betty, reached upward, and placed his gloved hands on Betty's shoulders. His large mongoloid-like eyes gazed deeply into her own.

Betty: He's putting both hands on my shoulders and is looking at me. And he says, "Child, you must forget for a while." He's telling me things.

As Quazgaa gazed at Betty, his head seemed to become fuzzy. It seemed as if she were looking at him but also *by* him. One of his eyes glowed white, but the other eye had a black eyeball. Two deep dark furrows above his eyes became very pronounced.

Betty: Quazgaa is looking at me with one white eye and one black eye. And this time, he looks just like a bee, with—somehow he's got two things, that come out like a bee on their head. Two, uh—not antlers; what are they, feelers or something? It's like I'm seeing past his head and I'm seeing him and he's like a bee, like a giant bee head with big eyes [*Sigh*].

Betty elaborated on this later, during debriefing.

Betty: He looked like a bee's face to me because his eyes got—you know, how a bee's eyes get the whole of the face almost? And it comes down very narrow....

Jules: Can you get that on paper?

Betty: I'm going to try—looked like feelers, you know, in the front.

Jules: Under the pear shape or on the outer surface?

Betty: Well, the eyes got huge like a bee's eye, like, you know, they were huge. Maybe it was because the skin might have been crinkled up and there was a *crease* that looked like feelers, like a bee. [See Figure 38.]

Ray: Did you feel dizzy or strange when he was looking at you in the eyes? He had his hands on your shoulders and was looking at you like this. As you were looking at him, did this sort of just change, like this?

Betty: Yeah, it changed, right. It seemed as if he were going deeper inside of me—my mind.

Then Quazgaa began to speak telepathically. It would be his farewell message to Betty. He would not be leaving the ship with her.

Betty: He says he's going to give me formulas. And he says until man finds those and understands those, he will not give any others.

Betty repeated Quazgaa's message to her.

Betty: He says my race won't believe me until much time has passed— *our* time.... They love the human race. They have come to help the human race. And, unless man will accept, he will not be saved, he will not live.... All things have been planned. Love is the greatest of all. They do not want to hurt anybody—but because of great love, they said: because of great love, they cannot let man continue in the footsteps that he is going.... It is better to lose some than to lose all.... They have technology that man could use.... It is through the spirit, but man will not search out that portion.

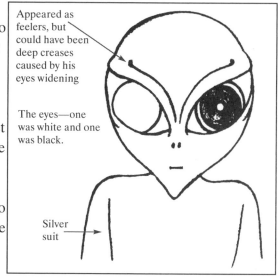

Figure 38: *"Quazgaa appeared like a bee."* *June 26.*

Betty began alternately pausing and then repeating Quazgaa's words. It was as if she had somehow been transferred back in time and was listening again to his enigmatical discourse.

Betty: Man must understand many of the natural things on earth.... If man will just study nature itself, he will find many of the answers that he seeks.... Within fire are many answers, within ashes—within the highest of the high and the lowest of the low are many answers.... Man will find them through the spirit. Man is not made of just flesh and blood.... It would be easy to hand them to us, but that would show that we are not worthy to receive those.... The knowledge is sought out through the spirit, and those that are worthy are given.... Those that are pure of heart, that seek with earnestness will be given.... Energy is 'round about man that he does not know of. It is the simplest form of energy. It is within the atmosphere—this atmosphere.... It has all been provided for him.... Many riddles will be given....

Those that are wise will understand.... Those that seek will
find.... They must remain hidden in this way because of the
corruption—the corruption that is upon the earth.... If they are
revealed outright, man would use it. [*Sigh*] He keeps telling me
of different things, of what is going to take place, what is going
to happen—they are going to come to the earth.... Man is going
to fear because of it.... Many are going to be astonished.... Yet
many are not going to be afraid because they have overcome
fear.

Betty continued to interpret and repeat the mental impressions that
the staring entity was transmitting to her mind. (We wondered about its
literal accuracy in light of the earlier misinterpreted "burned meat" incident.) Then Quazgaa closed his dissertation with a startling statement.

Betty: He says that he has had others here.... Many others have locked
within their minds, secrets.... He is locking within my mind
certain secrets [*Sigh*].... They will be revealed when the time is
right.... Again, he's putting both hands up on my shoulders. And
he's saying, "Go, child, now, and rest."

Quazgaa then took Betty into the small anteroom that she had entered
originally from outside the ship.

Betty: And he's—going through another room. It's raised up, and
it's going over to where I was to begin with. Some kind of an
up-thing. It is an opening.... And that's—we're up at that place
where I first came in. And the door is opening....

During debriefing, Jules asked her to go into detail about leaving the
craft.

Betty: Okay, after that cylinder (the half-cylinder room)— after that
purple pink light, we went through the door again and into that
same area where there's that big round elevator.... We went past
that again into that room where the dressing room was, over to
the side, where that hatch was. And the hatch—this time—was
sprung up and there was a huge, huge spring in the center—a
real huge spring. And there were four springs on the sides of it.

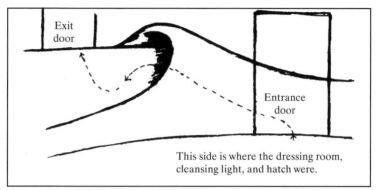

Figure 39: *June 26.*

Fred: You couldn't see where a door was until it opened?

Betty: Yeah, and over to the side was that other place where the bubble was, but we walked over to this side. We went through and it was a thing that swerved up and over, and then went in like that. [See Figure 39.] It was dark down in there.... And then, ah, we went over that somehow. I don't know how we got over that, but we got over that somehow and we went into the room where we had entered before. That room where there's a gully.

Ray: Now afterward—when you last saw Quazgaa, did his face change back to what he was before?

Betty: Uh-huh. He changed back. And then the door opened....

The door to the outside flashed open. Betty peered out into a mist-enshrouded night. The edge of her house protruded from a bank of round fog. She was going home! Betty, as usual, took up a middle position between two of her captors. The three of them floated down to the ground, one at a time, and proceeded toward the house in single file. As she later explained it:

Betty: And, ah, the two beings, rather than Quazgaa, went with me.... We jumped down and then—I saw the opposite side of the house, the flat wall of the house.

Jules: The left corner? The left rear corner?

Betty: No, the corner. Here is the corner of the house, right? I mean, here is the porch, and then a wall jutted out. A wall without windows jutted out. When we jumped out, I was facing that wall without windows, and we just jumped out and went around and just as if we really hadn't even moved!

Jules: What about the uniforms? Was there any change?

Betty: No, just the silver uniforms down into the boots.

Her alien companions carried the glowing white spheres.

Betty: There are only two with me now, and the one in front of me is carrying a round white globe.... And we're going now into the porch. I can see the old porch door. And we're going through it! And I'm following.... And we're going in—we are back in the kitchen.

A later debriefing would add important elements to this account.

Jules: When you got out of the craft and back on the ground, do you remember the conditions? Clear, bright night?

Betty: It was still misty. There was fog. You couldn't see off to the side. It was misty all around—you know, fog rising from the ground. But I could see the side of the house.

Jules: Did it feel cool, cold, or—?

Betty: A damp feeling.

Ray: Could you see the stars?

Betty: No.

Ray: You ought to check the weather report.

Jules: I should have gotten that report by now. I'll have to call and find out why.

Ray: I'm wondering if the mist had something to do with the object, or did the mist have something to do with the weather?

Fred: You told us about these white balls. Could you show us about how large those balls were?

Betty: There were two of them, and the one in back was holding it just like this.... He was just holding the small one.

Fred: The little one, maybe 4 or 5 inches in diameter?

Betty: About that size.

Fred: Did it glow?

Betty: It was light, but it stayed within itself.

Ray: Did it look like metal or glass?

Betty: Glass—it looked like glass. And he just held it in back of me like this. And the other one, he had the bigger one in his hand, and he rolled it. It rolled right over his hand and sat on the top of his hand. [See Figure 40.]

Fred: So he could, you say, roll his hand under it?

Betty: Yeah, it still stayed there, and he held it.

Fred: How large was that bigger one?

Betty: Maybe 8 or 10 inches in diameter.

Jules: Was this the same type of material?

Betty: Exactly the same as the other.

Fred: Okay, let's see now. The first ball, the smaller one—when did you first see that?

Betty: That was in that cylinder place, ah, when we were coming out. The other one went back over—uh, by that chair—that's where they were. They weren't with those balls when they *first* came into the house.

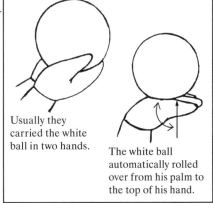

Usually they carried the white ball in two hands.

The white ball automatically rolled over from his palm to the top of his hand.

Figure 40: *June 26.*

Fred: So they took both of these balls when they went with you back into your kitchen?

Betty: The one in front of me had the larger one. The one in back of me had the small one.

When Betty reached this point in her original session, the hour was late, and she had a two-hour drive ahead of her. This seemed an appropriate place to end the session, so Harold awakened Betty from hypnosis. He gave her explicit instructions to remember where she had left off in the reliving of her unearthly experience, and we made hasty preparations to meet again in a few days.

"Today is the 26th of June 1977, at the New England Institute of Hypnosis. Session 11." Harold's voice seemed far away to me. June 25 was my wedding anniversary, and I was anxious to return home to be with my wife. Later on, we were going out to supper together to celebrate. This was just one of many occasions where the elusive UFO had interfered with family affairs. As each session got under way, it seemed as if my normal, everyday life was at complete odds with the paranormal world encountered within those four walls each week.

Abruptly, my daydreaming dissipated as Betty was given instructions to continue her account from where she had left off two days ago.

Harold: I want you now to take yourself back to the point that we left off this past Thursday where you were returned to the kitchen. Do you see yourself there?

Betty: Yes.

Harold: Please take over.

Betty: I'm standing in the kitchen and the—ah, two beings are there, and they're in silver suits. And we stopped. We're inside. And the being is turning and I can sort of...[*Pause*] I think he was on the inside as he turned. He has that ball, white ball in his hand. He's turning toward the right, and he's going over toward the pantry part there.

The alien being glided into the pantry area and stopped near the sink, where a partition divided the pantry from the kitchen. Betty watched him raise the larger white glowing ball before him. She gasped as her father shuffled out of the shadows. The entity had partially awakened him from a state of suspended animation.

Fred: Was your father in the kitchen?

Betty: He was in the kitchen, and I didn't see him because there—uh, where the kitchen sink is, there's a partition with an archway. He was over in the corner there, and I did not see him. But the being went over by the sink and raised his hand like this.

Fred: Is it your impression that your father was there all the time that you were in the ship?

Betty: Yes, that is my impression.

Evidently the ball the entity carried had some effect on Waino Aho's mental state:

Betty: He's raising the ball. And he's putting it on the outer part of his hand somehow...made it like, roll, over onto the outer part of his hand—top surface, not on the palm. And he's holding it up and pointing toward the window there. That's my father there! And he's just walking like in a daze—coming out and coming over. "What's the matter with him?" I asked him. He said, "He will be fine." And he lowered his hand and my father stopped there now. He doesn't look like he's aware of what's happening. He just sort of trudged out of there. And the being still has that round light on the top of his hand. He's like, gliding over and—he's got his hand down, like a—balance or something. He's balancing somehow, I guess, and he's lowering his hands again—lower.... And he's, uh, raising it and going into the other room, and my father is following him.

Betty shouted to her father, but received no response as he followed the little man into the living room.

Betty: "Are you all right, Daddy? Daddy!" He's not answering me. They're going into the other room, into the other room there. I'm just standing there. I don't hear any noise at all. Just standing in the kitchen. I turned and asked the other one, "What are they doing in there?" He won't answer me. He has that other smaller ball in his hand. He's just holding it out in the palm of his hand. Just standing there, still.

Then the first entity returned from the living room. He was not walking; he glided like a skater.

Betty: Here comes the other one back in now—gliding, seems like he's gliding. And he says, "Betty, now will you follow us?" And he got in front of me and turned. And he, too, has both hands holding on to it, both palms of his hands have that large ball. And they're walking into the other room.

Betty glided with them into the living room. Startled, she first saw Becky sitting mutely with a smile frozen on her face. All of her family looked like statues. They were completely unaware of her.

Betty: And they're still all sitting there motionless. Becky's sitting there, and she's smiling and grinning. She seems to be awake! She seems as if she's up, standing up, just smiling at me. Oh-h-h. [*Softly*] Just standing there.... Her expression isn't changing now. She seems to be frozen in that smile. Just standing up there, in the living room.

Betty's thoughts were suddenly interrupted by a voice in her mind.

Betty: And that one is saying, "Betty, you will have to forget this—you and your family—for the time being." I just keep on seeing Becky standing there smiling. "There are many other things that we have told you. They will come out at the *appointed time*. The book is over there," he says. And the book is over there—it's on the stand.

The entity was referring to the blue book that Quazgaa had given Betty earlier in exchange for her Bible.

The entity said, "We are now going to put you to rest."

"What about all of my children?" Betty asked.

"They have not been harmed," he answered. "We are just going to put them to rest, and they will be relaxed, and asleep."

One of the entities then proceeded to take the children to bed. The white glowing spheres seemed to have been employed as control devices.

Betty: And I see that one taking... [*Pause*] The little ones are standing up. They're standing up! And they're moving, but their faces seem as if they just don't know what's happening. They're just all getting in line. And they're.... [*Pause*] The being stopped and said he would be back shortly. The kids are just playing follow-the-leader there! They are just marching off, through the hall. And I can hear them on the steps, 'cause our stairs are squeaky. They're all going upstairs, except for me and my mother and father. And my mother and father are sitting on two sides here, and just waiting there.

Betty's eyes lighted on the small blue book lying on the stand.

Betty: And I turned to the other one and I asked him, "May I see that book while I'm waiting?" He still wouldn't answer. He just held that little ball in his hand. "May I see the book while I'm waiting?" He just won't answer. I don't even know their names. I don't know why Quazgaa didn't come back.

Suddenly the other entity somehow just appeared in front of Betty.

Betty: Oh! That other one is suddenly in front of me. I didn't even see him come in. He's just there.... He's holding that ball closer to my face.... [*Sigh*] He's taking my mother and father with him. And he's going...into the hall...into my bedroom [*softly*]. He's moving over now and wants to get after me now. And suddenly that one is in front of me again. Oop! Appeared, just appeared! He's raising up his hands.

One of the entity's hands held what looked like a glowing green candle. The other held the white glowing ball. Betty demanded to know who he was: "What is your name? What is your name?"

The entity said his name was Joohop.

"What is this all about, Joohop?"

"You will see as time goes by."

"And what about that blue book there," Betty repeated. "Is that for me?"

"For a time," Joohop answered.

"What is this all about?"

"Because of love. It's all about love. Man seeks to find out about our place...our ships...our knowledge."

"What about that book over there?"

"It is given to you for a while to grasp as much as you might grasp from it. There is writing there that will be discerned only through the spirit. And it's the writing of light. It can be understood only through the spirit. The other writing that is upon that is for man to seek and find out. There are formulas, and riddles, and poems, and writings—for man to understand nature, for he, too, is nature. He is formed from love, and love is the answer for man."

"Why is it man does not seek love all the time, Joohop?" Betty wondered. "Why is it?"

"Because man has separated himself. He has become dual—separation, duality. He has formed that other side. He has made it to happen. It was all good at one time. Even his choice was good at one time. He has separated it. Even in love there is some separation. Betty, follow me."

Betty: And he's taking me up into the hall and up the stairs. And I can hear the stairs creaking....

This detail puzzled me, and I mentioned it during a later debriefing:

Ray: What confused me is, if you were floating, how would you explain the stairs creaking?

Betty: I was floating.

Ray: Were you in control of your movements?

Betty: Until—until we started up the stairs into my room, I didn't seem under my own power. My mind was not under my own power, I don't believe, because I was following. Whatever he was saying, I was doing. When we got to the stairs, I was under my own power.

The entity did not return Betty to her own bedroom.

Betty: We are going around and around, and he's taking me into the white and purple room. He's telling me now that I will rest and I will forget all that has happened until the time is ready.

"Why must I forget?" she protested. "Why must I forget?"

"You must forget until the time appointed."

Betty: And he's raising that ball, and he's turning it over on the back of his hand again. And—I'm getting undressed and pulling the covers down and I'm crawling in bed just like I was a little child. I'm jumping in and crawling in, just like I remember seeing the little ones do. And I'm covering up and looking up at him, and he still has that big ball of light. And he's bending over me and he's waving his hand over my face. [*Softly*] I'm in bed and I hear whirring and whirring and—um, starting up something like a big motor or roaring. Like a whirring, roaring noise. I don't know. And it's coming over from the right-hand side, by Becky's little bedroom.... And it's not roaring anymore, just the—like a *"dink-dink-dink"*.... I don't know. There's just a—and I feel very relaxed and rested and, uh, I'm asleep.

Betty fell into a deep sleep. The next thing she knew was that it was the next morning. Familiar voices echoed up the stairs.

Betty: It's the next morning. And, uh, I jump out of the bed, and I feel very happy. I can hear the kids up already. They're downstairs. And I can hear my father talking with a couple of the boys. And he's talking in sort of a baby talk to Cindy. He always does that to her. And it's morning.

Betty awoke suddenly from hypnosis without aid from the hypnotist. Harold, in turn, put her back under hypnosis and then brought her out again without any stress.

The reader will recall that 11-year-old Becky had been briefly "awake" when the entities had first entered the living room. Almost immediately, though, Quazgaa had glanced at her, and again Becky lapsed into sleep. As she explained during hypnosis, the next thing she remembered was waking up in bed the next morning. At first, she thought that she had experienced a very frightening dream.

Becky: I'm waking up in the morning.

Joseph: You didn't see your mother and the beings leave the living room?

Becky: No, I didn't see her going anywhere.

Fred: When you woke up in the morning, were you still in the living room?

Becky: No. I was in bed.

Fred: Can you remember leaving the living room?

Becky: No. I woke up in the morning and came downstairs, and the kids were all fooling around.

Fred: How about the other kids?

Becky: And there's Cindy lying on the couch—no, Bonnie; it's Bonnie lying down on the couch.

Joseph: Did you fix breakfast? Or did Mom have breakfast for you? What happened?

Becky: No. Mom must have had it ready for us, 'cause we had pancakes.

Debbie: (sitting in on session) Was your mother up?

Becky: Yes, Mom was up. She was in the bathroom—'cause Scotty wanted to get into the bathroom. He was down in front of the door.

Fred: Did you talk about what had happened the night before?

Becky: No. I didn't tell my mom that until about three days later.

We wondered if Betty had noticed any physical marks on her body after her UFO experience.

Ray: There were no marks on your body, your navel, your nose? You never felt any pain there—anything like that?

Betty: I never checked. I couldn't. With seven kids, I had to keep well.

Some of our questions assumed she had total recall of the experience on the following day. We tended to forget that prior to her recall via hypnotic regression, Betty had remembered little about the UFO incident. Other than vague memories of the creatures entering the house, the rest of the experience had somehow been blocked out of her conscious mind.

Ray: How much did you remember of what happened when you got up in the morning?

Betty: I don't know. It's too long ago.

Fred: I'm interested in whether you went out the next morning to look in the backyard to see if there were any signs or impressions on the ground.

Betty: No, but I just thought recently about that back hill. We were trying to grow grass there, and grass would not grow on that hill. We thought it was because of the children always passing through from school. And we would stop the kids and ask, "Would you please use the sidewalks?" You know, Becky? Do you remember that?

Becky: Yeah, because they walked through on a path.

Fred: The grass grows there now, doesn't it?

Betty: It's all dug out. The whole hill was dug out. But we even were going to call the principal because the kids just—you know, they had one line. We didn't want to be mad about it or anything, but we were going to call the principal to see if they could somehow speak to the kids to please use the sidewalks. You know, I was making the garden and we were trying to grow grass.

Jules: How much of an area was it? Just a path width?

Betty: No, that whole hill would not keep grass.

Ray: Had it before?

Betty: Yes. There was just the path coming down, and then the whole thing started to get all bare, like patches. That's why we were throwing grass seed on there.

Ray: So, when you wrote to Dr. Hynek in 1975, how much did you remember about the incident?

Betty: The pulsating light was the first strong thing. That was the strongest thing I remember—the pulsating light. For a long time, that's what I remembered. And then I started to remember the part about them coming in—you know, the beings coming in.

Ray: And so, that was about when—1967, 1968, 1969?

Betty: I think it was about 1969.

Ray: How about your father? Did your father ever mention these
            strange creatures he saw out the window and ask you where they
            came from, what they were doing, and so forth?

Betty: No.

Ray: So, the first time you really got any confirmation that he saw
            anything at all was just recently?

Betty: When I called up and asked him if he remembered anything
            about the UFOs and about the experience that I had, he said
            no to begin with. And then afterward, he told me yes, but he
            did not want to get involved in it. I told him, "Daddy, then why
            did you tell me no, you didn't see it? Why didn't you tell me at
            the beginning of it?" And he said, "I don't want to get involved
            in that stuff!" And my mother is scared stiff of it. When we
            were down my sister's house and she learned Jules had come
            up, she was thinking that an *actual UFO man* was coming up,
            you know. She said no. She said, "Don't send him up to my
            place at all!"

Ray: As far as you know, she doesn't remember anything at all?

Betty: No.

Ray: What are you going to do now that all of this has been brought
            to your conscious mind?

Betty: I really don't know what to do about it, Ray, I...I'll tell you how
            I really feel. I feel a little threatened— because of my faith.
            I don't want it to fall upon my head if it is [*Pause*].... I don't
            know. I feel a great responsibility and, uh, I shouldn't feel a
            responsibility because my faith is that Jesus takes the burden
            from me. And yet, there is.

Ray: If you accept at face value the messages they gave you, why do
            you feel threatened? They seemed to reassure you that they are
            part of what you believe.

Betty: Maybe because of—it's just that so many people...telling me about coming down to be hypnotized, "Oh, Betty, don't do that. That's against God. It's in the occult realm." It's even stronger in the churches.

Ray: They told you that you were going to forget about this incident for a while—or for a time, *your time.* Do you feel that we are doing the right thing in trying to bring this out? Do you think that *this* is the right time?

Betty: Well, I feel that when I sent that letter to Dr. Hynek, a whole weight went off my back. I felt that I searched as much as I could search, and it had me in a state of anxiety. I couldn't find out any more—I figured, here's somebody that really is interested in finding out about it. They have the knowledge. They're educated. They are really going to spend time searching out the thing. I felt relieved, I figured, this was it—I just figured at least, the burden was off me and I really felt better before God. I felt as if, "Lord, I've done all that I'm able to do in searching out the thing." Exactly when was the date that I sent that letter to Dr. Allen Hynek?

Jules: Here's the letter—August 20, 1975.

Fred: Do you think that we as investigators should be working with you to try to help bring out this knowledge? Is that a desirable thing to do?

Betty: If this is what you would like.

Ray: You don't feel any inclination to do a book?

Betty: Well, you know, as I said, a book if it can help people. But also I'm worried about the effect on my faith and what people are going to say, and what they're going to think. And religions are going to get uptight about it.

Ray: Do you think that this is the end of the affair, now that it's all out?

Betty: No, I don't think it's the end of the affair. I know there's so much locked up inside of my mind. I don't know what it is. *I* *know it's not the end.* I know that there are many things in there, and they probably will just start coming out. I know they are going to be easier to come out now than they ever were before. *I don't know what they are, but I know that it's going to come out when I least expect it.* I don't think I'll be afraid this time.

I have added the emphasis to portions of Betty's last statement—which, as the reader will soon see, was only too accurate!

Betty: If suddenly something comes to me, I'll write it down and get in contact with you. I think that I would rather stay in contact with you than get involved with any new investigators, because I feel as if you are my friends.

Betty was preparing to move to Florida at that time.

Jules: Well, even when you're in Florida, I'd like to call you once in a while and see if you've got anything new.

Betty: Fine, that's fine. Well, I'll tell you if I get new things. I will automatically send them to wherever you want me to send them. As things come out, I'm going to write them down.

Ray: Should we consider this the last session for our report? If something else comes along, fine, but let's get this whole thing documented.

Fred: I think we want to get it down, read it all through, and then ask more questions.

Jules: One thing that we should do, if possible, is have her put back under hypnosis and see if she could look at the blue book and come up with some kind of formulas, proof, or....

Fred: Yeah, I was hoping you had kept the book for a number of days and had a chance to look at it.

Our debriefing session ended. Betty was exhausted from the ordeal we were putting her through but agreed to attend two more hypnotic/debriefing sessions. We wanted to find out just how long she had kept the cryptic blue book and how much she had learned from it. But we were to find out that the aliens had other plans for us. They would intervene directly!

C•H•A•P•T•E•R 9

➤ Messages for Humankind? ◄

It would be a full three weeks before we again submitted Betty to hypnosis. On the following week, tragedy struck when Peter Neurath, one of our investigators, was stricken with a heart attack and died. Needless to say, no session was held that week. Arrangements were made to conduct further lie detector tests with Betty and Becky on July 9, the following Saturday, and the next two hypnosis/debriefing sessions (sessions 12 and 13) were scheduled for July 16 and 23.

Of particular interest to us were the little blue book and the messages given Betty by the aliens. On July 16 the 12th session began with what had now become a rather routine matter. Betty was soon under hypnosis and was regressed to the time when she and the entities were in the living room after her return to the house. We attempted to probe her mind for the messages given her by the aliens. One of the investigators had asked a question:

David: (investigator) At any time, Betty, did either Joohop or Quazgaa give you any predictions for the future? Things that would happen on earth?

Betty: Yes.

David: Can you reveal these now?

147

Betty paused. Her face became contorted. It looked as if she were struggling against someone or something that was taking control of her speech facilities!

Betty: They—have things—in control. —They—are—in—the heavens. They—have—powers.—[*Sigh*] —They—can make—you— think one thing—and yet—mean—another.—I don't like them controlling my words!

Joseph: You are still in the living room talking to them.

Betty: I know I'm *there*, but I'm *here* also.

Somehow Betty had been whisked from a past event that she had been reliving to the *present* time. No one in the room had suggested that she do this. Stunned, we could not understand why or how she had abruptly moved into the present time.

David: Do you feel they are controlling your words *now?*

Betty: They were, and I don't like it. I don't like them controlling my hands either. [*Sigh*] Oh, my arms and hands!

Joseph: Are they doing something to your arms and your hands?

Betty: Yes, they are, and I don't like it!

Joseph: What are they doing to your arms and hands?

Betty: I don't know. They're doing it just like they had me before.

Joseph: They are restraining them?

Betty: Yes.

Her hands and her feet felt restrained, as they had before on the examination table in the UFO.

Joseph: What does it feel like, Betty?

Betty: Feels like I can hardly feel them. They are so numb that I don't have any feeling, like I'm stuck to something.

Betty's struggle was in vain. Whatever had sought to control her had the upper hand, and at this point, she started talking in an unknown language—mechanically, as if someone else were speaking through her! The following phonetic rendition represents the closest approximation of this language that I could derive from listening to the original tape recording. The total passage took about 35 seconds to deliver.

Betty: Oh—tookfirah bohfitfitah mawhfilah dfih dfiwa ma her dfih okaht tfiraht [*Sigh*] nawrlahah—tfitrah aw—hoe—hoe marikoto tfitrah etrah meekohtfi- trah etro indra fikreeahlah [*Sigh*].

Fred: Betty, what are you saying to us?

Betty: I'm just saying it. I don't know what they're saying to you.

Fred: Are you repeating things that they are saying to you?

Betty: I don't know what it is. They're just saying it to me. I don't know what they are saying.

Betty again broke into a foreign language. Then: "Base 32—Base 32—[*Sigh*] Signal Base 32."

Fred: Betty, can you tell us any more about that? Does that refer to a number or a place?

Betty: [*Softly*] I don't know. [*Softly, to herself*] Is it a place? Is it a place? Curvature, curvature. Sombleado. Star Seeso. Sombleado. Star Seeso. [She continued with more strange language.]

David: Betty, is this a message we are supposed to understand?

Betty: I don't think it's from the book. I think it is coming from something.

Fred: Is this a message that you got then? Or is this a new message?

Betty: No, I didn't get it then. It must be from *now*.

Fred: Do you feel you're in contact with them now?

Betty: I don't know, but my hands feel like it's the same as it was then. So do my feet and my legs.

David: Betty, is there something that they want us to understand right now?

Betty: [*After a pause*] Yes.

David: Do you know what it is? Can you tell us what it is?

Betty: [*Pause*] Something about scientists must bury the past.

Fred: Say some more. Tell us some more!

Betty: There is an even flow. There are waves that are being sent out. And there are old walls that need to be broken down.

David: Can you tell us more?

Fred: Does this relate to the formulas that they gave you, or is this different?

Betty: This is different, something about circling the plain. Circle the plain, P, L, A, I, N. Uh—count three and four, count three and four. Counting three and four is very important.

Fred: Can you tell us what the three and four relate to?

Betty: It's something about a door, and it's going to be opened. Oh, my hands!

Jules: Betty, you mentioned Star Seeso. Is that a place?

Betty: Yes.

Jules: Is it in our galaxy?

Betty: No.

David: Is that where they're from?

Betty: No.

David: What does that mean to them?

Betty: It means something about a two and a four and zero, zero, line under zero, zero, zero, line under zero, zero, line under—it keeps going on!

David: Betty, did they ever tell you, give you, the name of the place where they are from?

Betty: I can't pronounce it.

David: Did they ever show you a map?

Betty: All I see is a line straight down and—one, two, three, four, five lines. There's something like [*Pause*] circled. I don't know what it is.

Jules: Can you draw us a sketch of it?

Betty: If I can remember it, I'll try and draw it.

Fred: Try to fix it in your memory so you can draw it for us later.

Betty: There's an anchor there.

Joseph: Are you still in the living room, Betty?

Betty: No, I'm right here.

While we changed our recording tape, Betty was taken out of hypnosis. While the tapes were changed in several strategically located recorders, we asked a few questions.

Joseph: Did you see a map?

Betty: It was a weird thing.

Joseph: Was it a chart, a map? Where did you see it?

Betty: I've just now seen it.

Joseph: It's in your mind now, or was it a few minutes ago?

Betty: A few minutes ago, when I was in here, in this room. I was no longer back in that time. I was here. Whatever that was that came out was not from that time. It was now—and there's an anchor.

Jules: You mean like a metal anchor? A sea anchor?

Betty: Something. It's an anchor. I can't explain, somehow an anchor.

Betty was then returned to a hypnotic state and was asked if the aliens had anything to do with a recent power blackout in New York City.

Betty: They have powers. They can control the wind, and water and even lightning.

David: Did they tell you what the purpose of the blackout was?

Betty: It was to reveal to man his true nature.

David: What is man's true nature?

Betty: Man seeks to destroy himself. Greed, greed, greed, greed. And because of greed, it draws all foul things. Everything has been provided for man. Simple things. He could be advanced so far, but greed gets in the way. Freely it will be given to those that have loved. [Again Betty spoke in a strange tongue.]

Fred: Betty, is this a message for us?

A feeling of tension filled the crowded office as again Betty's face became twisted and words forced themselves out through her reluctant lips.

Betty: Even—now—you—cannot—see.—Even—now—we speak.

David: We are trying to see. Do you have a message for us?

Betty: You—try—to—seek—in—wrong—directions.—Simplicity—
'round about you.—Air—you breathe—water—you drink—
[*Sigh*]—fire—that—warms— earth—that—heals.—Simplicity
ashes—things— that—are—necessary—taken—for—
granted.—Powers—within them—overlooked.—Why—think—
you—are able—to live? Simplicity.

David: Betty, are you telling us this? Are you interpreting this for us?

Betty: No, I'm not telling you those things.

David: How do your arms and legs feel right now?

Betty: Terrible.... That feeling in my hands—to hold my hands down.

David: Do you feel that the beings are using you?

Betty: Yes, they are. [*Softly*] And I don't know how they're doing it.

David: What do they want us, as seekers of the truth, to understand
right now?

Betty: The truth—freedom—love—to understand man's hatred—to
deal with it righteously.

David: Are they trying to protect man from himself? Is that true?

Betty: No, and yes. No, because—because other worlds are involved
in man's world. Man—is very—arrogant—and greedy—and he
thinks—that all worlds—revolve around—him.

David: But not all men think this way.

Betty: Only—because—love is present.

Fred: Will the blue book help us to understand the message?

Betty: You—would—be—in—just—as—much—darkness—about—
the—blue—book.—First—seek—out—the—simple forms—
of—your—selves.—Man—is—arrogant—because—his—
image—makes up—everything—that—is—condensed—and—
pride—dwells—there—because—of—the—image—that—
man—has—been given. [*Sigh*]

Fred: Do the beings want us to understand? Does Quazgaa want us to understand?

Betty: Quazgaa—is—just—an—official officer—under—the—clan—like—many—others.

Fred: But my question is, do they want us to understand and to gain knowledge?

Betty: Yes.

David: What is the clan?

Betty: It will not be told right now, they said.

Jules: Where is Seeso?

Betty: Far, far, past, twenty-four zero, zero, zero, zero, zero, zero, zero, zero, zero, zero, zero, zero, zero. I don't know how many zeros.

Joseph: Betty, where are they from?

Betty: They said, you will know the truth, and you will know once you find the truth.

Joseph: Betty, what is the truth?

Betty: I've told you the truth before. Jesus Christ is the truth. He is the answer for mankind. He's the only answer.

The investigator had asked Betty, not the alien, what the truth was. Betty, predictably, answered the question from the perspective of her religious faith. Fred quickly realized Joseph's mistake and addressed his question to the entities who seemed to be controlling Betty.

Fred: I have a question for the beings. I would like to know if they are willing to help us to find knowledge. Can we find out if they are willing to help us?

The apparent answer via Betty had chilling implications.

Betty: You—would—not—have—gotten—this—far—nor—gained—this—much—information—had—we—not—desired—to—help—you.

Fred: Then I would like to have some indication of their help for us to proceed further. What must we do for the next step? How do we proceed further?

Betty: Search.

Joseph: In what direction?

Betty: That—which has been given to you—seek—search. We—shall—help—reveal—certain—pieces—of—the—puzzle—will—be—fitted.—Try—to—understand—yourselves.—Seek—spiritually.—Seek. —Doors—have—been—left—open—to—you.—The great door—shall guide.

Joseph: What is the great door?

Betty: It is the entrance into the other world. The world where light is.

Joseph: Is that available to us as well as to you, Betty?

Betty: No, not yet.

Joseph: Is it available to you?

Betty: Yes.

Joseph: Do you understand what is on the other side of the great door?

Betty: Yes, I understand and believe in it.

Joseph: Can you help us to understand?

Betty: If you will accept it.

Joseph: Will they permit you to guide us?

Betty: No, they want to guide.

David: Betty, we would like to try, then, to pursue this truth. We would like you to go back again to the evening of the incident.... Pick up the story where, ah, Joohop was taking your mother and father to bed. Do you remember that point?

Betty: I remember it, Dave, but I can't go back there right now.

David: You can't?

Betty: They have my hands and my feet and my legs.

Joseph: Are you being requested to continue the conversation?

Betty: It must be, because they're applying more pressure on my hands and my feet.

David: Okay, then. You don't have to go back right now.

Jules: The twenty-four zero, zero, continuous zeros. Is that in miles, meters, light-years?

Betty: It is in sunbursts.

Joseph: What does the term "sunburst" mean, so we can understand it?

Betty: It is something about the darkness that is left there after the sun has been exploded, I guess, or something or other. I don't know. [*Weakly*] They won't tell me.

Jules: Are they referring to our sun as we know it?

Betty: Yes, our sun. Sunbursts.

Jules: Is the sun a key to the truth?

Betty: Yes.

Joseph: Is this sun explosion in the future or in the past?

Betty: The future and the past are the same as today to them.

Joseph: Does time exist?

Betty: Time to them is not like our time, but they know about our time.

Joseph: They recognize time as our dimension, but they have something else, through time?

Betty: Yes, they can reverse time.

Joseph: They can reverse our time?

Betty: Uh-huh.

Fred: Are the beings able to come here again?

Betty: They travel freely. They travel freely throughout our whole earth.

David: Can they travel inside the earth?

Betty: Yes, their density is much different, although they have metals that they cannot penetrate. They have to have those metals.

David: Are those metals in the earth?

Betty: [*Softly*] Some of them.

David: Is that one reason they're here?

Betty: Mmm, no. But some of the metals in the earth are enough to carry man to where they are. Then, when they get to their certain station, they are able to subtract ores from that planet for the use of going on further.

David: Have they been visiting the earth for very long?

Betty: Since the beginning of time.

Joseph: Our time?

Betty: Yes.

David: Can they travel freely throughout the stars?

Betty: Certain ones.

David: Are these stars nearby to the sun and the earth?

Betty: Yes, and they are beyond.

David: What do you mean by "beyond"?

Betty: Beyond ours there are others, but they are in a different plane. They're in a heavier space.

David: What do you mean by "a heavier space"?

Betty: They're in a heavier space than we are.

Joseph: Why are they restricted to some stars and not others?

Betty: Why are we restricted to earth and able to go only to certain stars, and not others?

Joseph: Is that the answer or is that another question?

Betty: That is the answer and the question.

Joseph: Betty, do they have enemies as we have enemies?

Betty: There is one planet that is an enemy, and also many men are enemies, only because they do not understand.

Joseph: Men of this earth, you mean?

Betty: Yes.

David: Betty, are there many of these clans or races visiting the earth right now from many planets?

Betty: Yes.

David: How many?

Betty: Seventy.

David: Seventy different planets or races?

Betty: Races.

David: Do these races work together?

Betty: Yes, except for the offensive one.

Joseph: They come from different planets, then? They don't come from the same planet? Is that correct?

Betty: Some. Some come from realms where you cannot see their hiding place. Some come from the very earth.

Joseph: This very earth?

Betty: Yes, there is a place on this very earth that you do not know of.

Fred: Can they see the future?

Betty: Definitely.

Fred: Can they tell whether we are going to come up with an answer?

Betty: The answer is here already.

Joseph: When will we recognize it in our time?

Betty: When you give your heart over.

Joseph: Does that mean that each individual being will recognize it at a different period?

Betty: When the heart is given over, each one will see it.

Jules: When the heart is given over to what?

Betty: To love and truth.

Joseph: Does that mean that some people have already seen this since many, many years gone by, and some will never see it?

Betty: Yes, and it is sad, because it was there for all mankind.

Fred: Betty, what is your personal function in revealing this?

Betty: They said that they have chosen me to reveal it because of the initiation, because of going through what I had gone through, because it was planned.

Jules: Why were you chosen?

Betty: Because I did not object.

David: Betty, have other people like yourself been involved in being taken on board their craft and examined?

Betty: Yes, but they quiet them. They tell them to be still. It's hidden within them. As time goes by, mysteries are going to be unlocked from man. These people are very afraid.

David: Did they tell you how many such cases there have been of people being taken on board?

Betty: Many, many, many, many, many. Many, many cases. Many, but only a few have gone to the fullness.

David: Have some of these people been taken back to the planets of the beings? Have some earth people been taken back?

Betty: Yes, and they're going to return, and people are going to be afraid because of it.

David: Were you taken to their home planet?

Betty: [*Long pause and weak voice*] I was taken to the high place, higher than their home planet.

David: You mean a more important planet?

Betty: It is not a planet, it is a *place*.

Because Betty was showing signs of fatigue, Harold released her from the hypnotic trance, and we proceeded to question her. We were curious as to why she had not remained reliving the past as she had been instructed.

Joseph: How did you get back to today? You were back 10 years ago.

Betty: I know. I was back there in the living room, and suddenly I was in here.

Joseph: Was that because of our questions, or don't you know?

Betty: I don't know.

David: Betty, I tried to get you back to the time of the blue book, and you felt that *they* wouldn't let you?

Betty: I couldn't.

David: You couldn't? You felt that they were preventing you?

Betty: Uh-huh.

It seemed as if the aliens had prevented us from learning certain information by intervening directly in Harold's office!

David: What else did you feel at that time?

Betty: Just that they had hold of me and they pressured me. Somehow—holding me down. It was pressure.

David: That was in addition to the weight in your arms and legs. Was that with you at other times when you were under hypnosis?

Betty: No, at certain times.

David: During these times, was it at all similar to the weight you felt in the craft?

Betty: Yeah.

David: Do you feel as if that weight is an indication of them controlling you somehow?

Betty: Yes.

Joseph: Would that be an indication that *every time* you feel that weight, you are getting a message directly from them?

Betty: I don't know, 'cause I don't feel that weight. I didn't feel that weight when I was lying down.

Joseph: But that was communicated to you directly. In all other cases when you felt the weight, you were communicating to other people. You were communicating with *us*.

Betty: Yes.

Joseph: Perhaps, when you are talking to us, you are being used as a translator. You are conveying a message.

Betty: This isn't a message to me.

Joseph: It isn't?

David: Is it a message to us?

Betty: It must be. It isn't to me.

Jules: Do you remember anything about this alien planet?

Betty: No.

Jules: You just know somehow that it was alien to the beings?

Betty: They said there is one planet that is alien.

Jules: It is hostile toward them?

Betty: Yes.

David: Do you feel that we are on the right track, as far as our questions go? Trying to get them to talk to us through you? Do you feel that they want that to happen?

Betty: I don't know.

Joseph: Did you feel uncomfortable during that?

Betty: Just when they put the pressure on me, or whatever it is.

Joseph: Do you feel mentally comfortable?

Betty: No, I feel tired.

Joseph: Yes, but that's because of hypnosis.

Harold: How are you feeling, Betty?

Betty: Pretty good.

David: Do you have any apprehension right now about us trying to regress you to a time immediately after the incident so that we can pursue information about the blue book?

Betty: No, I don't have any problem.

David: But at the time, you felt that they were preventing you from going back.

Betty: I couldn't go back.

Joseph: Was that because in asking the questions, we reverted you back to *now*?

Betty: I don't know. I wish I had the answers.

David: Is this it for today as far as hypnosis goes?

Harold: She has had enough hypnosis.

At that point, we decided to go after more "hard" data.

Fred: The Bible that you handed to the leader, Quazgaa—what happened? Did they give you back your Bible?

Betty: I don't know, because all I remember seeing is that blue book there. So they must have kept it.

Fred: They must have kept your Bible?

Betty: Well, I don't know if it's my Bible. We had many Bibles. Becky couldn't find her Bible afterward.

Becky: I told my mom that it was missing.

Fred: Do you remember when?

Becky: Sunday school. I took it to Sunday school every Sunday.

Fred: It could have been her Bible, and they probably took it. Is that what you think?

Betty: This could be, because I didn't see it back on the end table. Only the blue book was on the, uh, end table.

In other words, the blue book had remained in Betty's house *after* the aliens' departure! In the next session, we decided to go back in Betty's memory to see what, if anything, she could recall of this mysterious document.

➤ The Blue Book ➤

We remembered that three days after the event, Becky had approached her mother with her own memories of the incident.

Betty: It was about two days later that Becky came to me with her dream, and she—two or three days later, she told me about it.

Harold: Why did you wait so long, Becky?

Becky: Because I thought it was a dream. And then I thought, well, with dreams, something in here will get over it. It's just a dream. But it upset me, and after three days it was upsetting me so much I had to tell Mom, 'cause it was just bothering me too much. I was scared.

Ray: Did you remember that something had happened?

Becky: I told her that I had a dream. I told my dream, and she told me that was true, that really happened...but not to tell anyone about it, and don't worry about it.

Betty: And it hit me then that "That was no dream, honey. That really happened, but don't tell anybody."

Now, in the 13th session, we returned the hypnotized Betty to the moment when Becky first related her dream.

David: Becky first mentioned the dream she had that related to your incident. Can you go back to that time now?

Betty: It was about three days later she mentioned it. She came to me and she said, "Mommy, I've had a strange dream."

David: When was this? In the morning?

Betty: Yes, and she told me what she had seen. I said, "Shush, shush, quiet. Don't scare the kids." And she said "Why?" And I said, "Come here." And I brought her into the bedroom and said, "Mommy is going to tell you that it wasn't any dream, honey. It really happened. There were some strange things in the house, but don't tell anybody, will you?" And she looked at me funny and she said, "You mean what I dreamed was true?" I said, "Yeah, but don't be afraid, 'cause Jesus is with us." I said, "I'll show you." And I did take the blue book out.... I'm feeling very cold right now.

David: Are you feeling cold when you touch the book?

Betty: No, I just feel cold because of telling you about it. It gives me goose bumps. I'm all right now. Maybe it's because I wasn't supposed to show anybody the book.

David: Do you remember showing it to anybody other than Becky?

Betty: No, I just see us—she sitting on my bed, and I'm going to the closet.

David: Is this the closet in your bedroom, where you kept the book?

Betty: Yes, and there is a noise in the kitchen, and so I put it back and I closed the closet. I went out into the kitchen and I told her, "Shush, just wait a minute, honey, I'll be right back." I went out into the kitchen, and it was just Jimmy and Mark coming in for a drink of water—I went to get the book again and showed Becky. I told her, "Now, don't tell anybody, will you, honey, because it's very important. It's from Jesus." Becky's face just lit right up. She was beaming. She was so happy and excited over it.

David: Did she say anything about seeing the blue book earlier?

Betty: Yes, she said, "That's what they gave you, Mommy. I remember, that's what they gave you." And I'm getting the chills again for some reason.

Joseph: Do you think that they wanted you to show Becky the book?

Betty: I wasn't supposed to show anybody.

David: See if you can remember as clearly as you can the last time that you saw the thin blue book they gave you. Can you try to remember that?

Betty: The *last* time I saw it?

David: Yes.

Betty: The last time I saw it all alone?

Once again, we realized we had "called" for the wrong time period and decided to follow Betty's lead.

David: You're all alone? Where were you?

Betty: In my house.

David: Can you tell us about this time?

Betty: I have just locked the front door, 'cause the kids have gone to school, and my mother and father have gone back home, and I'm sitting at the table and I'm opening it up.

Fred: How long after the sighting was this day when you last saw the blue book?

Betty: Ah, I think it was...[*Pause*] I think it was nine days.

Fred: Do you know what day of the week it was?

Betty: It was a weekday, because I know I went to get it, and it wasn't there, and I was shook up. I thought maybe the kids had gotten a hold of it. I couldn't touch the book on Sunday because they were around. When they went out to play, like on Saturday, I could take a look. It was really bothering me 'cause I wanted to study that so much and to see what it was. My father and mother went home, and that Monday they were gone and my kids were in school, and I felt, now I can do it.

Ray: Betty, where had you kept the book prior to locking the door and going to the kitchen table to look at it?

Betty: I hid it in the closet.

Ray: Why did you hide it in the closet?

Betty: I don't know.

David: Did they tell you to hide it in the closet, or to keep it hidden?

Betty: Yes, they said that.

David: Did they tell you why they wanted you to keep it hidden?

Betty: It must not be seen by any that were not worthy.

David: Did they give you a reason why they didn't want you to show the blue book to anyone?

Betty: Because it was for initiation, and Becky was too young and had to go through too many things yet in order to see it.

David: Why did they pick you?

Betty: It was a book of initiation of mysteries of everything that is. It is because of things I have gone through and yet have stood fast.

Joseph: Were you supposed to study it?

Betty: I was supposed to look at it and grasp as much as I could possibly grasp for the future.

Joseph: Is that the information that you have locked in your memory that you were to release in time?

Betty: It is a portion of it, but the biggest portion is what was told me from Quazgaa and Joohop.

David: After your parents had left and you were able to sit down with the book, what did you first do?

Betty: I was just at the kitchen table there and I was just opening up the book.

Jules: Did you look at the cover to see if there is any symbol on the cover?

Betty: There is something there. [*Whisper*] What is it? It's like in the very center. It's very thin. Thin gold. It just looks Egyptian.

Fred: How many pages are in the blue book, and did you look through all of them to see how large it was?

Betty: Around forty thin, thin papers.

Joseph: Are they numbered?

Betty: No.

Fred: Are they printed on both sides of the sheet?

Betty: No, that's what's strange. On the other side, it's a glowing white.

David: The other side of every page?

Betty: It seems it from here, but it seems as you get toward the black writing, it seems as if...[*Pause*] unless it just comes through from the other page. It's so thin. For some reason, I'm very close to the book. I'm looking down about 10 or 12 inches from the book, and there is strange writing in it and numbers.

David: Is this writing you're describing on the first page?

Betty: No. I'm in between the pages.

David: What do you mean—that the symbols are *in between* the pages?

Betty: It's maybe about the fourth or fifth page.

David: Had you just opened the book up to this page?

Betty: I opened it to more pages than the beginning, because the first three pages were just white light—glowing. There are all sorts of symbols.

Betty attempted to describe the strange script in terms of familiar things.

Betty: One comma-dash like a curleque of some kind. A sweeping under in a circle, and then two lines close to each other with a kind of a rounded line on top like a—you know, like a...with two sides. A zero with a dot and some kind of a line on an angle going through that with a little flag-type thing on the line.

Fred: Are there pictures in the blue book? Illustrations? Or is there only writing?

Betty: No. There are diamonds with a dot in the middle. There is something like a staff and there are arrows. There is, uh, something that is on an angle and—it's a rectangle on a side, and it goes out.

Fred: Betty, can you understand this writing that you see?

Betty: No, I'm just looking at it.

Fred: Do you feel that the blue book is giving you information? What is the value of the blue book to you in terms of what does it do?

Betty: It's mysterious because of the strangeness of it.

David: Were you able, then, at this time to look at every page in the blue book?

Betty: At this time, I'm just seeing a pyramid again.

Fred: Is that in the book?

Betty: Yes, a pyramid, but a strange-type pyramid. It has a chute on it, and it has an arrow, some type of an arrow. It's all strange. All strange. It's like, ah, takeoff things for airplanes or something like pyramids with, uh—it's just hard to explain it.

Fred: Can you fix this in your memory so you can draw it for us later?

Betty: I'll try to.

David: Try to remember what was on each page of the blue book. Try to write it down and draw it for us after the session.

Betty: I will try. I would prefer if possible to do it now while I am seeing it.

Jules: You mean now while you are under hypnosis?

Betty: Yes.

Joseph: You want to do that now, Betty?

Betty: Yes, if I can have the power in my hand. [Her hands were rigid while under hypnosis.]

Jules: Here is a pen. Would you rather have a pencil?

Betty: I will have to first somehow be released. My hand.

Harold released Betty's hand as requested. Betty proceeded to draw symbols on a pad of paper held by the hypnotist's assistant. She kept her eyes closed while writing.

David: Are all these symbols that you are drawing on one page?

Betty: Yes.

David: Do you remember which page it is?

Betty: No.

David: Are you feeling right now that any of these symbols are more important than other ones?

Betty: There is a mechanical thing that I couldn't draw.

David: That's okay. Maybe you can draw it later. Are there any other symbols that are important? More important than others?

Betty: The written meaning to it cannot be written by our words.... It's unspeakable in words, our words. It can only be seen through symbols.

David: After you were through looking at the book, what did you do with it?

Betty: I put it up, and I took my Bible and lay down on the sofa.

David: Where did you put the book?

Betty: I put it back up in the closet, underneath a box.

David: That's where you had been keeping it?

Betty: Yeah.

David: Okay then, proceed. You took your Bible and lay down on the sofa.

Betty: Yeah, and I was praying to God to reveal to me what it was all about. I prayed to Jesus that I didn't understand and that He would have to help me.... [*Pause*] And then certain words started coming, and at first I didn't do anything about it.

David: Is this the first time that you got these words or knowledge when you'd been sitting with your Bible?

Betty: I started getting those things like different words.

David: But was this the first time?

Betty: Yeah.

David: When did you next look in the closet for the blue book? Was it the same day?

Betty: No, I think it was the next day, and I was scared 'cause it was gone and it had been entrusted in my care.

David: This bothered you?

Betty: Yes.

David: Didn't they tell you that you would only have it for a period of time?

Betty: Yes, that's right. They did tell me that.

David: Did they tell you how long it would be?

Betty: They said it would be 10 days.... [*Pause*] That's right; they said it would be 10 days that I would have to look at it.

Joseph: Did they tell you they were going to take it back?

Betty: Yes, they said that they would give me so many days to look at it.

David: On this day that you looked in the closet and found that it wasn't there, do you remember what day it was? What day of the week?

Betty: It seems like—[*Pause*] it seems to me like a Tuesday. It could have been a Thursday.

David: Why do you say Tuesday?

Betty: Because the day before, the kids were at school.

David: Couldn't it have been a Wednesday?

Betty: Wednesdays I went shopping because I would always look for Wednesday bargain days to save money.

Joseph: Well, when was the last time that you went to pick up groceries—before you lost the book?

Betty: It seems as if I stayed in the house. It seems as if I didn't want to leave it. I didn't want to leave that book alone there.

Joseph: So then you didn't do any shopping until after the book was gone?

Betty: That's right. I don't think I did because it was too important. I wouldn't leave that alone.

Joseph: Did you go shopping the following week?

Betty: I must have, but my heart wasn't in it.

David: Did you spend a lot of time with the blue book each day until you found it was missing?

Betty: Yes, I did spend time with the blue book. It's strange, because it was mostly my Bible that I usually spent time with, and why I would spend as much time on that blue book is strange because the Bible is all-important to me.

Fred: Did you go to church between the time of the sighting and the date at which you last had the blue book?

Betty: [*Softly*] No.

Joseph: How did they recover the book?

Betty: I don't know. It's gone.

David: Betty, on the day that Becky mentioned the dream to you—did you actually hand the book to Becky?

Betty: She touched one of the white pages. Her hand seemed to glow from it. She touched the second white page of the three white pages of the beginning of the book, and her little hand glowed from it.

David: What did she say?

Betty: She just said, "Look, Momma!" And I said, "I know, I know." And again, I'm getting goose bumps.

David: Are you getting cold?

Betty: A little cold now.

David: And after you and Becky were finished looking at the blue book, what did you do with it then?

Betty: My hands and my feet are beginning to feel that feeling!

David: Are they?

Betty: That feeling in my hands again. Oh-h-h-h! They're starting to hold my hands down again!

Betty realized that the aliens were again taking control of her. Were there some things about the blue book that the aliens did not want us to know? We attempted to find out if this was the case.

David: Do you feel as if they have a reason for doing this, Betty?

Betty: I don't know what it is, but they're doing something to me again.

Joseph: Now?

Betty: Right now!

Betty suddenly began speaking in an unknown tongue and sighed deeply.

Fred: Betty, can we contact the beings today?

Betty: Yes.

Fred: Will you ask them if they'll answer some questions for us?

Betty: They said, "If it is in the scope of realism."

Fred: Okay, would you ask the being you're in communication with what his name is?

Betty: Andantio.

Fred: Andantio?

Betty: That's what he says, or what the word is.

Joseph: Where is he from?

Betty: He is from the same place as those that have been before him.

Joseph: What is the name of the place?

Betty: I can't pronounce it.

Joseph: Can you write it? Can you spell it?

Betty: It begins with a Z.... [*Pause*] It isn't like ours. There's too many consonants and very few vowels in it, and I can't pronounce it.

Joseph: Can you spell it? Can you see it? Can you see the word?

Betty: No, he's saying it.

David: Is it one word, or two or more, or can't you tell?

Betty: It's one word.

Again, Betty started speaking in the strange tongue.

Fred: Andantio, may we speak with you *directly?*

Betty: Not at this time, he says.

David: Does he give you a reason why not at this time?

Betty: Because you are not ready.

David: Can he tell you why we're not ready, or what we need to do to prepare ourselves to be able to communicate with him?

Betty: He can see that you are serious. Simplicity has got to be there. Minds are open, but there are walls there—walls that have been caused by knowledge. We would not understand what he would tell you, and it would be a waste until you find the simple things.

Joseph: Can he tell us something that we would understand?

Betty: Know yourselves. Please, please, please know yourselves.

Virginia: Betty, could I ask you about the symbols you described last week which you got from this being?

Betty: Yes. Is it the line down with the lines through and the circles with the anchor to the right?

Fred: I have a question for Andantio. I want to know if he is familiar with the formulas that were given to you.

Betty: Those formulas are very simple.... They are the building blocks to a higher way.

Fred: I'd like to ask some questions regarding the first formula.

Betty: It has to do with a liquid that life has been removed from. It is stillness. Are you able to understand this? It has stillness within it. It will not wave or move—no vibrations. It's pure.

Fred: I would like Andantio to come here so we could talk with him directly. Andantio, will you come here *now?*

Betty did not say a word. The room was silent and we glanced about apprehensively, half expecting Andantio to materialize! Finally, Betty broke the eerie silence.

Betty: I asked him if he would be willing to, and he will not answer.

Jules: What are the walls and barriers that we have to overcome in order to communicate with him?

Betty: Again, [*Softly*] know yourself. You think that you know yourselves, but you do not know yourselves. You do not know what you are made up of. You do not know the powers that you possess. You do not know the extensions of love.

Fred: I don't understand what Andantio would have us do in order to better communicate with him. I think he will have to come here if we are going to have better communication. I'd like to understand more about how to bring that about.

Betty: You would worship him if he was to come here, and that is not his way. You would be in awe of him. It is his way because he is just a servant and a messenger.

Ray: Can he show us some proof that he is really communicating through you in this room—something that we would accept without hesitation as proof that he actually exists and is talking through you?

Betty: The world seeks proof. They cannot see with the spiritual eye. Only those that are worthy will see.

Ray: But man's mind has been so created that in every other area of life, he has to accept or reject what he feels is reality on the basis of some type of proof. Can he understand the limitations and show us some kind of proof?

Betty: He understands the limitations. The proof came long ago and still is—he could do all sorts of tricks, but it would not be his way.

Joseph: We're not looking for tricks. We don't want tricks. We're looking for information.

Betty: He knows that you are looking for information.

David: Betty, is Andantio of the same race as Quazgaa?

Betty: Yes, he is.

David: Do you feel that they are messengers of the Lord?

Betty: I believe it now, yes. If I did not believe that they were messengers of the Lord, then I would not give my will over to be used.

Fred: Andantio, is there a more favorable time or place to communicate with you?

Betty: I can communicate with you when you are sitting at work, when you are driving in your car.

Fred: What is the most favorable time and place?

Betty: Time with us is not your time. The place with you is localized. It is not with us. Cannot you see it?

Fred: I still would like to have you come directly to communicate with us telepathically now. Won't you please do that?

Betty: Would the vessel tell the maker what it prefers to have in it?

This cat-and-mouse game continued until it was quite apparent that no further information could be obtained from the quizzical Andantio. It was obvious, too, that he was deliberately blocking our efforts to secure further information from Betty pertaining to the blue book.

The question remained as to whether we had actually communicated with an alien, or with Betty's subconscious mind. But in any event, Betty and her family were in the process of moving to Florida, and reluctantly we decided to call the sessions to a halt.

Betty Andreasson was a simple, unsophisticated country girl. Her childhood was happy and carefree, but the years that followed her marriage had been alternately laced with joy and sorrow. A marital problem developed early that Betty patiently bore for years. Shortly after her 1975 letter to Dr. Hynek, the marital problem intensified, and she and her husband agreed to separate. When we first met Betty, she had shouldered the responsibility of raising her remaining family single-handedly for well more than a year.

She had hoped for the problem's solution and eventual reconciliation, but it did not work out. Reluctantly, Betty had initiated divorce proceedings. She sought a new life and was preparing to move her family to be near relatives in Florida.

The round trip to Dr. Edelstein's office was more than four hours. The long hypnosis and debriefing sessions, coupled with the burden of remembering the unnatural experience, left Betty mentally and physically exhausted. But packing, leasing her house, and managing everyday household affairs had not dissuaded her from cheerfully attending each hypnosis/debriefing session.

We marveled at the tenacity of this woman. In spite of the pressures of a busy schedule, it was obvious that she was determined to find out what had happened to her.

Then, after sessions had been discontinued and just several days before Betty was to depart for Florida, her father was hospitalized with cancer. After going into shock during kidney dialysis, Waino Aho died on August 27. After the funeral, Betty sadly left for Florida to look for a new home for her family. I would not see her again until October.

It was time, as they say in the intelligence community, to make an estimate of the situation and begin the task of evaluating the immense amount of data collected thus far.

C·H·A·P·T·E·R 11

➤ Preliminary Correlations ◄

The reliving of the traumatic experience by hypnosis and the occurrence of several family tragedies, coupled with Betty's impending divorce, had affected the lifestyle of the principal witness. Nonetheless, this had not negated our overall character check, which provided ample evidence that both she and Becky are honest and emotionally stable persons.

Harold Edelstein had no previous experience with UFO investigation. As the series of hypnotic/debriefing sessions progressed, he seemed genuinely impressed. But for the most part, he kept himself in the background and became directly involved only when necessary. He was careful not to let his words and thoughts influence Betty in any way.

It wasn't until session 12, on July 16, 1977, that Harold made any definitive statement concerning the provocative case. After this session, he took the investigators aside.

"Okay," Harold said. "I'm going to tell you what I honestly think. I think there is substance here, but it can't be pushed because you'll frighten her."

That wasn't the question on Fred Youngren's mind: "What do you think we can believe of what we're hearing here?"

"I don't know if you can believe everything, but I believe wholeheartedly that in many instances, she believes what she's telling you. The facial expressions and breathing can be changed," Harold explained, "but a person has to really *believe* in what they are telling you in order for them to change. Play that tape back. Now at certain points, when I said to you, 'Get a picture,' her face was twisted up on the side. It didn't even look like Betty. Am I right?"

"Yes," Joseph Santangelo admitted. "She looked like she was in agony."

"Now, these things are very important. Another thing that leads me to believe that a good share of this may be true is that she comes up with different things at different times. As she goes over it, it is just as though she were having a recollection of something."

In sum, Harold concluded that at times, Betty and Becky appeared to be reliving an experience that was very real to them, and he advised us to make sample videotapes at some of the sessions. He believed that a good portion of the experience reflected actual reality, but he confessed he could not deduce how much was real or imagined. This deduction, he stressed, could only be made by comparing the Andreasson Affair with other reports for similarities. Such a comparison would be an intricate part of the last procedure employed in our investigation: analyzing all collected data pertaining to the case.

At the beginning of our investigation, all we knew was that Betty's alleged experience had occurred early some time in 1967—and interestingly enough, 1967 was a vintage year for UFOs!

The longest sustained UFO sighting wave in recorded history had begun in the spring of 1964. At the time, I was chairman of the Massachusetts Investigating Subcommittee for NICAP (National Investigations Committee on Aerial Phenomena). For the year 1966 alone, our subcommittee had logged a record number of 43 local reports evaluated in the unidentified category. In fact, UFO researchers all over the country shared a common frustration: There were too many high-quality reports and not enough trained investigators to document them. By January 1, 1967, local reports dropped off to a few per month, and it appeared that the long-lived UFO wave was diminishing. Then, without warning, UFO activity again increased dramatically.

On January 15, 1967, a bright red oval object ringed with a white halo circled a home in Boxford, Massachusetts, at 3:00 a.m.

Three days later, shortly before midnight, a bright flash lit up the skies over the sleeping village of Williamstown, Massachusetts, just as an electrical power failure crippled the area. Four persons approaching the darkened town sighted a domed glowing object hovering just off the highway. As they passed by, the object rose into the air and buzzed their car.

Two nights later at Methuen, Massachusetts, three persons—Kim, Janice, and Ellen—were on their way to pick up a friend for a local basketball game. The lonely street was bordered by woods, fields, and very few houses. Reaching the top of a hill, they were shocked to see up ahead a string of about 10 bright glowing red lights that were moving over a field just off the road to their left.

"What's that?" Janice asked.

"It must be a helicopter," Ellen replied.

Kim laughed. "It must be a UFO or a flying saucer!"

During my interview with the witnesses, Ellen remarked to me that at this point, "all of a sudden, it wasn't funny anymore." The object stopped moving, and they were closing on it rapidly. Kim slowed the car. Simultaneously, the object seemed to swing around, as if it were "spinning on its axis," and revealed lights of a different color and configuration.

At that point Kim pulled the car over. Janice said, "Let's go look at the helicopter." She and Kim wanted to get out of the car, but Ellen didn't. All of a sudden, the car stalled and the lights went off. Then *nobody* wanted to get out of the car! "Truthfully," Ellen told me, "I was too scared to carefully observe the object."

Kim told me that, during this juncture in the sighting, she had opened her side window in order to get a better look at the object: "The lights and our radio all went off at the same time. After this, I tried to start the car twice while the object remained stationary. Thinking that the lights and radio would be drawing too much power from the battery, I shut the light switch and the radio off. Then I tried to start the car again. It did not start."

In the meantime, the house-sized object hovered a mere 300 feet away. Kim told me that "it was like the color and texture of Erector Set material," and formed an inverted bowl shape around the lights. Ellen cowered in the back seat. (Curiously, the generator panel amp dimly pulsated off and on until the craft began to move away slowly.) Abruptly, it picked up speed and streaked away along its original flight path—where it was seen by another car full of people. The whole incident had lasted only a few minutes.

The strange sightings continued. On February 16 two policemen in Amherst, Massachusetts, responded to a UFO sighting reported to the station. Dumbfounded, they watched a glowing object like a bright white light bulb hovering in the night sky. A weird swishing sound emanated from it. Amazed, they watched it eject a small red object before accelerating out of sight over the horizon.

On February 17, at about 7:00 p.m., a salesman for Flying Tiger airlines was driving along Route 93 near the junction of Route 495 in Andover, Massachusetts. Cars slowed down and warily passed under a huge lighted object hovering directly over the road. Frightened, he, too, passed under the silent craft, which was larger than the width of the entire superhighway! In the early morning hours on that same date, shortly after 1:00, several people residing in Dorchester, Massachusetts, were awakened by an extraordinary whirring sound. Glancing out windows, they sighted an object that looked like a cymbal with a dome on top, with purplish lights around its perimeter. It hovered at treetop level over an elderly peoples' project before moving way and out of sight.

On February 26, in Marlboro, Massachusetts, a husband and wife were awakened at 2:00 a.m. by a strange sound. When they got out of bed to investigate, they sighted a white glowing egg-shaped object swinging like a pendulum in the sky.

On March 1, at 7:25 p.m., witnesses in Sharon, Massachusetts, were amazed to witness a noiseless white glowing oval object that maneuvered near their home. It left a white glowing fuzzy trail in its wake.

According to the U.S. Weather Service, March 8, 1967, was a clear, cool night. Visibility was 12 miles. In Boston the thermometers read 28 degrees Fahrenheit. A recent snowstorm had left a beautiful blanket of white velvet draped over the fields and trees. A couple I'll call Mr. and Mrs. William Roberts of Leominster, Massachusetts, got a sudden inspiration to go for a late-night scenic drive through the countryside. After driving for an hour and a half, they started home.

At about 1:00 a.m., they entered the town of Leominster, where, as Mrs. Roberts later told investigator Frank Pechulis, "We suddenly came across a very thick fog and had to slow our car to a real low speed for safety reasons."

"As we passed the cemetery," Mr. Roberts continued, "I noticed what looked like a large light to my left. I asked my wife if she saw anything, and she said no. I was certain that I had, and decided I would look again." Mr. Roberts, thinking that the light might be a fire and that the fog was smoke, turned his car around and drove back into the mist. This time, they both saw the light. The bright glow was not from a fire, but from an object glowing in the air directly above the cemetery! At that point, Mr. Roberts lowered his window and excitedly told his wife, "I think we have something here!"

He parked the car broadside to the hovering object, which hung in the air a bare 200 yards away. Bright as an acetylene torch, it was shaped like a flattened egg and emitted a sound like a dynamo.

Against his wife's wishes, William got out of the car. Excitedly, he raised his hand and pointed it at the blazing object. Simultaneously, the automobile lights, radio, and engine ceased functioning. At the same time, Mr. Roberts received an electrical shock. Almost instantaneously, his body became numb and immobilized from head to foot, and his arm was thrust back against the car by some unseen force, hitting the roof so hard that an imprint was made in the ice and snow. "When the car went dead," Mrs. Roberts interjected, "I was yelling for Bill to get back in the car, but he did not move."

"I was unable to move," Mr. Roberts told the investigator. "My wife was in a panic. My mind was not at all affected. I just couldn't move!"

When he did not respond to her screams, she slid across the seat and tugged at his jacket through the open window. He could hear her begging him to come back inside, but he couldn't move a muscle. He was totally paralyzed from head to foot.

Mr. Roberts recalled, "I was there 30 to 40 seconds before the object moved away. It moved quickly at an ever-increasing speed, not instantly." Abruptly, their car's lights and radio came back on. The humming object had accelerated upward and out of sight above the dense fog patch. (On the following day, at Andover, Massachusetts, witnesses would sight a strangely lit silent object hovering about one thousand feet above the grounds of a country club.)

Incredible reports by credible people poured in. Later on in the year—on July 27, about 1:00 a.m.—a group of amateur astronomers saw a wingless, cylindrical object maneuvering over the darkened countryside of Newton, New Hampshire. (Two of the witnesses were trained observers and had received training in aircraft identification in the military.) As the object moved back and forth near the field in which they had set up a telescope, it responded exactly to signals flashed to it with a flashlight by one of the three witnesses.

Some UFO reports included the sighting of occupants by the witnesses. Several months prior to the Newton, New Hampshire, sighting, a former U.S. Coast Guard pilot and owner of a small airport in eastern Massachusetts was awakened by a weird humming sound. Thinking that an aircraft might be attempting an emergency landing, he leaped out of bed, flung on robe and slippers, turned on a bright yard light, and hurried outdoors to investigate.

The half-awake—but highly trained—man was totally unprepared for what greeted him. Hovering just 25 feet over a small pond between the house and the airport was a strange, silent aircraft. It was not a helicopter. He later told me it looked like "two shallow metallic saucers, one inverted upon the other, with a transparent canopy situated on its topside." Elongated vent-like holes spaced evenly around the object's rim emitted a soft orange glow. A softer, greener light bathed the interior of the canopy, revealing two humanoid creatures who stared down at him!

Thinking that it must be an experimental aircraft in trouble, he cautiously walked toward it, yelling and waving his arms. Instantaneously, it moved smoothly and silently away from him, stopping again over some gasoline pumps and aircraft at the edge of the runway. The curious witness ran around the pond and again headed toward the hovering craft, waving his hands at it as he approached. Abruptly, a swishing and loud whirring sound came from the object, and the orange lights began spinning around its circumference. Slowly and deliberately it tilted back before shooting away at fantastic speed. Simultaneously, the bright yard light dimmed to practically nothing during the object's initial acceleration, but quickly returned to normal as it moved away. All that was left behind was a smell reminiscent of burned matches lingering in the night air.

Others were to have similar experiences. On November 2, 1967, two Native American youths were driving south on Highway 26 near Ririe, Idaho. At about 9:30 p.m., a blinding flash of light erupted in front of their car, then quickly dimmed to reveal an oval object with a central dome. The dome was transparent, and they saw that it contained two small humanoid creatures who stared down at them.

About a month later, on December 8, 1967, in Idaho Falls, Idaho, a young woman stepped outside to look for a friend who was on her way to pick her up. She noticed a patch of light reflected off the snow. Glancing up to see where it was coming from, she was horrified to see a circular object hovering silently in the overcast sky. As she stood awestruck at the sight of it, the object tipped and rotated, revealing a central transparent dome. In the dome she could make out the distinct outline of two humanoid figures gazing down at her. As the object moved away, she panicked and ran into the house. At its closest, she estimated that it was only about 300 feet away and about 100 feet off the ground.

Significantly, a great number of 1967 UFO reports involved sightings in upper central Massachusetts. A number of reports of objects hovering over freshwater ponds came from Phillipston, Royalston, Orange, and Tully, Massachusetts. Several objects were reported to have had a central dome. But the surge of UFO activity that reverberated into 1967 merely bracketed the incredible experience of the Andreasson family. What they had experienced was but a logical extension of all other aspects of the UFO phenomena—that is, a CE-IV: contact!

At that time, all we knew was the year of the sighting: 1967. But later, during the course of the hypnosis/debriefing sessions and other interviews, attempts were made to determine the actual date of the experience from the witnesses' statements. From Betty's overall testimony, we were able to start narrowing down the exact day.

Betty: It is 1967...the lights went out. My father and mother were staying with me. Husband in the hospital from a car accident. Snow, little bit...it's cool, misty...fog rising from the ground....

With this information in hand, we checked hospital records, local power company records, and detailed weather records kept by a weather station in Ashburnham. Hospital records show that Betty's husband was transferred from a local hospital to a Veterans Administration (VA) Hospital near Boston on January 23, 1967. He was not released until March 17 of that year.

Ashburnham Municipal Light Company records show that a power failure occurred in Betty's neighborhood on January 25, 1967. It was traced to a defective primary loop cutoff, which was replaced on the following day. (Unfortunately, the *time* of the failure was not recorded.)

The U.S. Department of Commerce weather station at Ashburnham recorded that a *trace* of snow was present on the ground between January 23 and 27, 1967. (The ground was *covered* with snow from January 28 through March 17, 1967. Depths ranged from 2 to 29 inches.) Weather records also revealed that the night of January 25, 1967, was misty.

Betty: Three days later, on a Saturday, Becky mentioned a strange dream. Mother and father went home that Monday.

Saturday would have been three days after a Wednesday. The evidence was strong that the UFO experience had taken place on Wednesday night, January 25, 1967. Much of Becky's later testimony under hypnosis substantiated this date.

Becky: Father in hospital.... It got real dark. Think I'm 11. Birthday long time ago...cold outside...ground cool and damp.... Traces of snow...grass dead.... Path was muddy.... Bozo on TV.... Saturday was three days after.

Weather records indicated that on January 25 there was a thaw with temperatures rising to 54 degrees Fahrenheit. That would explain why the path was muddy. And a check of TV records confirms Becky's statement that Bozo the Clown was indeed on television the evening of January 25.

During Becky's initial recall, it was very disconcerting to us when she described herself and her friend eating *apples* from the orchard!

Becky: We both climbed up and sat down in the tree talking and eating apples.

Harold: Are the apples hard?

Becky: Yeah, real hard.

Apples seemed hardly in season during January, and we felt that Becky was imagining or mixing up this aspect of the account. Even though she talked like an 11-year-old while regressed by hypnosis, we sometimes treated her as the 22-year-old adult we saw at the present time—and in doing so, perhaps we expected too much of her. In this instance, however, she may have been giving us an accurate description.

On December 24, 1977, I visited a local apple orchard during a thaw. It was a balmy day with a temperature of about 50 degrees Fahrenheit. There were dried-up apples *on* some of the trees, and piles of both decayed and *firm* apples *under* the trees.

I picked one up and took a bite out of it. It tasted all right. Later, on January 28, 1978, I sent field investigator Jules Vaillancourt to the orchard behind the house formerly owned by the Andreasson family. Under the tree, Jules found apples that had frozen and thawed—and they were edible. It looks as if we underestimated Becky.

While under hypnosis, both Betty and Becky were asked what *time* the incident started. Because Betty had not noticed the time, she could only guess: "I don't know, but seven o'clock keeps going through my mind."

Becky, however, could see the clock in the living room when the lights began flashing through the kitchen window: "They got there at twenty-five of seven."

When Betty was returned to the house and entered the living room with the entities, she had noticed the clock: "It is ten-forty.... It's dim, but the hands look like ten-forty—in between ten forty-five and ten-forty."

Inquiries revealed that the Andreasson family had eaten early suppers, between 4:00 and 4:30 p.m., during this period, so that the children might be fed and prepared for bed before Betty left to make her nightly visit to her husband at the local hospital. Betty ceased these visits when her husband was transferred to the VA Hospital near Boston on January 23, 1967, but the habit of early suppers was still maintained on January 25. Using information extracted from the hypnosis sessions, the scenario following on pages 187–188 could be constructed.

Another aspect tending to verify the account of the witnesses was that some portions of the story would be correlated with real-time events. We have just seen that their description of environmental conditions and circumstances corresponded to reality. Of course, the date and time of the incident were derived from this data. Interestingly enough, the present owner of the house in Ashburnham confirmed that because of the lay of the land, a dense, local fog tended to form behind the house. Weather conditions on January 25, 1967, were conducive to the misty conditions Betty described. Indeed, if not for the dense fog on that evening, the landed UFO could have been observed by others from neighboring houses.

In addition, measurements of the backyard demonstrated that an object of the dimensions Betty described could have landed only where she had reported seeing it on the ground. True to her statement, at the reported landing site, it would have needed adjustable landing gear. A check of the interior of the house (granting allowances for known renovations) also corresponded to the descriptions given under hypnosis.

Having established the estimated date and time of the Andreasson Affair, we continued on to complete a detailed analysis of the remaining data. During this study, we encountered startling similarities with other Close Encounter UFO reports, in more than a dozen important categories.

Becky			
4:00	to	4:10	I was outside playing and we had to come in…
		4:35	for supper…
4:35	to	4:55	After supper...had to do dishes.
4:55		5:05	After I did my dishes, I could go outside.
(Sunset 4:48)			Just a little bit longer before it was
5:10		5:10	real dark...I had to stay in the yard.
			And then Mom called us in...and then we just stayed in the house.... The TV was on...I went upstairs to my room.
		5:20	I was probably there about ten minutes
(Bozo program ran from 4:30 to 5:30)			and I came downstairs and I was watching TV. The kids were watching
(4:30	to	5:30)	Bozo the Clown.
5:30	to	6:35	We were just watching TV.... And then Grammy was saying something.... Mom broke in saying "hush, hush."... And there was that reddish light outside.
		6:35	
Betty			
6:35	to	6:55	We were in the kitchen...about twenty to twenty-five minutes.
		6:55	I went in the living room...they followed.
6:55		7:00	I passed...Bible to the leader.... He gave me a book.

		7:00	**Becky** When I woke up again, it could have been seven.
		7:00	**Quazgaa** Would you follow us?
		7:00	**Betty** All right.
7:00	to	10:40 10:40	(The abduction period) (The return) It is ten-forty...by that clock.

1. The Vacuum-like stillness at the outset of the UFO experience

The sudden stillness that enveloped the Andreasson house has been reported in connection with other UFO reports as far back as 1933 (that is, *prior* to the influx of modern UFO sightings in the 1940s). APRO reported a sighting from the year 1933 that took place between Lehighton and Nazareth, Pennsylvania. A male motorist stopped his car to examine a strange violet glow in a field. Approaching the eerie light source, he found it to be emanating from a round object resting on the ground. While in the vicinity of the object, he neither saw nor heard a living thing and stated that the silence was "deadly."[1]

Another report from this period comes from Canadian UFO researcher John Brent Musgrave, who documented a sighting which took place in the summer of 1933 at Nipawin, Saskatchewan. Several persons jumped into a truck and drove to an area where strange lights had been seen to descend. In a field they sighted a large oval-shaped object, supported by legs, with a central dome. About a dozen short figures could be seen moving around the craft. They reported that "all was a strange sort of quiet."[2]

We see this same peculiarity manifested in some modern sightings. On November 5, 1974, at about noon, Harry Pinhorn observed a strange gray object hover over the factory at which he worked in Lisarow, Wyoming. He stated that a strange silence that engulfed the area caused him to notice the object: "I looked up at the trees because the birds had all suddenly gone quiet and there it was."[3]

At 8:45, on a clear night, January 21, 1977, Robert Melerine was paddling his boat quietly up the Dike Canal in St. Bernard Parish, Louisiana. Abruptly a glowing object moved rapidly toward him and hovered overhead, engulfing him in warm light. He stated that there was a complete silence: "No wind. No frogs croaking or ducks calling. Silence."[4] Three boys at Salisbury North, Australia, had a similar experience shortly after. A low-flying object cast a beam of light at their bicycles on May 27, 1977. Investigator Colin Norris stated that "the *stillness* that the boys noticed...is consistent with many other reported sightings."[5]

At 5:00 a.m. on June 24, 1977, a married couple living in Lubbock, Texas, were awakened by the sudden movement of their dog. Puzzled by the dog's antics, the wife got up and went to the door. She stated, "When I first woke, I could hear the sound of about a million crickets in all the trees here. But almost immediately, it was just deathly quiet—not a sound." A glowing object hovered outside over her neighbor's house.[6] Still another case of this sort occurred on October 9, 1977, at 8:30 p.m., in Walcott, Iowa. Holly Prunchak, a security guard at the French-Hecht plant, watched a strange, lighted oval object descend over farm property across the street. The Center for UFO Studies dispatched veteran investigator Ralph DeGraw to conduct an inquiry. DeGraw learned that "all the ambient animal noises (cattle and crickets) went quiet when the object was in view."[7]

An identical effect was noticed by witnesses to a sighting that took place a decade earlier in Brookfield, Wisconsin. On August 12, 1967, at 2:30 a.m., a sleepy man and wife glanced out the window to see what their German shepherd was barking about. Shocked, they saw an oval object hovering at ground level over an adjoining pasture. A sharply defined beam of light emanated from the craft and the dog stopped barking. Everything became strangely silent. The usual night sounds of insects and animals ceased abruptly. "There was dead silence outside."[8]

Note that the reported silencing effect appears to be connected with certain lights from the UFO, just as it seems to have been in the Andreasson Affair.

2. The concurrent electrical failure

Earlier in this chapter, I mentioned the localized power failures sometimes associated with UFO sightings. These included the area surrounding Williamstown, Massachusetts, on January 18, 1967, and the case involving the manager of a small airport in eastern Massachusetts when his yard light dimmed concurrently with a Close Encounter UFO sighting.

Our local team of investigators has investigated a number of these so-called electromagnetic (E-M) effect cases, some of which have been quite spectacular. Walter Webb, assistant director of Boston's Hayden Planetarium, documented such an event that took place in Dorchester, Massachusetts, on April 24, 1966, at 5:00 a.m. An oval domed object, encircled with red lights, hit and shook an apartment complex. A simultaneous power failure was traced to a burned cable near the object's flight path.

3. The concurrent TV interference

UFO interference with radio and TV has been a common occurrence over the years. Two cases will suffice to illustrate this effect:

1. November 5, 1957, Ringwood, Illinois. UFO followed car to town. TV sets in town dimmed, finally lost picture and sound during same period of time.

2. November 10, 1957, Hammond, Virginia. Police chased UFO. TV blackout in city.[9]

4. The physical appearance of the entities

In 1971, I managed to secure a number of pages from a thought provoking textbook employed by the United States Air Force academy for a course relating to UFOs. In a section captioned "Alien Visitors," the following excerpt seems highly pertinent to the discussion at hand:

> The most stimulating theory for us is that the UFOs are material objects which are either manned or remote-controlled by beings who are alien to this planet...The most commonly described alien is about three and one-half feet tall, has a round head, arms reaching to or below his knees, and is wearing a silvery space suit or coveralls. They have particularly wide (wrap-around) eyes and mouths with very thin lips.[10]

This description is also borne out in civilian sources. Concerning height, an analysis of UFO occupant reports prepared for the Center for UFO Studies[11] states that 27 such "dwarf" cases were reported in 1973. One such case allegedly involved another family's CE-IV on October 16, 1973, at Lehi, Utah. Using hypnosis, Dr. James Harder, consultant for the Aerial Phenomena Research Organization (APRO), elicited from one of the witnesses the following description: The beings were slightly over four feet tall, very thin, with large slanted eyes. Their arms were long and their hands gloved and claw-like, with a diminutive thumb. They were wearing what appeared to be glowing clothing with Sam Browne belts!

5. The entities' ability to float

A number of UFO reports describe *floating* entities associated with the observed craft. The Ririe, Idaho, case (alluded to earlier) involved two UFO occupants gazing down at the witnesses from the object's transparent central dome. One of the humanoid creatures left the hovering craft, and "with a *floating* movement like a bird" descended to the door at the driver's side of the automobile.[12]

At Brands Flats, Virginia, on January 19, 1965, the witness reported seeing three small beings float down to him from a hovering object. (This case will be discussed further later, as it bears other similarities to the Andreasson report.)

Air Force Sergeant Charles L. Moody is a member in high standing of the United States Air Force's Human Reliability Program. Candidates for this program are carefully screened by psychiatrists for emotional disorders during the process of selection for this elite group. I mention this because Moody reported to APRO that he was abducted from his automobile outside of Alamogordo, New Mexico, during the early morning hours of August 13, 1975. He said of his dwarflike captors: It's going to sound ridiculous and I hope nobody sends me a straitjacket, but these beings did not walk, they *glided*.

6. The luminosity of the entities' uniforms

Although Betty did not remark on the glow emitted by the entities' uniforms until later, when she was inside the dark tunnel, other witnesses have reported the same thing under ordinary nighttime conditions. For example, the aforementioned Lehi, Utah, incident also involved small beings with glowing clothes.

Another case involved a young man on March 28, 1967. At about 2:25 a.m., he was returning home to Munroe Falls, Ohio, from the night shift at the Lamb Electric Company in Kent, Ohio, when he spotted a luminescent UFO hovering off the left side of the road. Shocked, he saw four or five small creatures moving extremely rapidly back and forth across the road. They were like little people with disproportionally large heads and no distinguishable features. They were emitting the same colored glow as the UFO.

Yet another report of this type originated in Goffstown, New Hampshire, on November 4, 1973. While investigating another incident in that area that had occurred a few days previously, UFO field investigator John Oswald and I were checking the police blotter for other reports. We came across a file card that read, in part: "Subject called this H.Q. and reported that there were small silver subjects running about his yard.... Patrolman Wike advised that Mr. Snow had seen something and that this was not a figment of his imagination."[13]

What did Mr. Snow see? We investigated and found out.

Shortly after midnight, the Snows were startled by a brushing sound against their house. Their German shepherd, Miko, began whining. Mr. Snow got up to let the dog out and was surprised to see light shining under the bedroom door from the corridor outside. Opening the door, he found the light was coming through the kitchen window from the outside.

Miko was crouched on the floor near the door, emitting a low growl. Her teeth were bared and the hair on her back bristled. Mr. Snow told me that his first thought was that there was a fire burning outside. He walked up to the back door, parted the curtains, and peered out. What he saw so amazed him that he just backed away from the door in utter astonishment. Looking out again, he saw that the diffuse white glow was emanating from two *self-luminous,* small silver-suited creatures gathering something from the ground at the edge of the nearby woods.

7. The physiological effects: suspended animation, numbness, prickling, etc.

Another recurring characteristic of UFO Close Encounters is the temporary paralysis of witnesses. On June 15, 1964, in Lynn, Massachusetts, an intermittent roaring sound caused the witness to run outside to investigate. A bare 20 feet away from him, a domed oval object was slowly ascending over the driveway. He stopped dead in his tracks. Concurrently, he felt a tingling sensation that began from his feet and ran upward through his body. He wanted to move but found himself completely immobilized until the object left the area.

Just one day before, miles away in Dale, Indiana, Charles Englebrecht was watching TV. At about 8:55 p.m., a brilliant light source passed by the kitchen window. As he got up to investigate, the TV and house lights went out. Going outside, he was astounded to see a glowing object hovering at the edge of the backyard. As he started to approach it, he abruptly became immobilized by what he described as "being shocked by a small electrical charge."[14] The Leominster, Massachusetts, case described earlier in the chapter involved a similar effect upon the witness as he left his automobile and pointed at a nearby hovering object.

One of the most sensational sightings of this type was investigated by NICAP and actually evoked a visit to NICAP headquarters by a CIA agent requesting information on the case. On January 19, 1965, a man then living in Waynesboro, Virginia, was working by himself at the Augusta County Archery Club off Route 250, near Brands Flats. At about 5:40 p.m., he sighted two silvery oval objects approaching in the sky. One quickly descended and landed about 50 feet away from him. From it emerged three humanoid beings dressed in silvery suits. As the entities approached him, he found that he could not move a muscle. After looking him over, the creatures reentered the object through a door that appeared to "mold itself into the ship." The object then ascended and flew off.[15]

8. The telepathic communication with the entities

While returning home from work during the early morning hours of November 2, 1973, Mrs. Lyndia Morel also had a Close Encounter while passing through Goffstown, New Hampshire. A UFO paced her car. It came so close that she could see a figure with slanted eyes staring at her from a transparent section of the craft. As she told investigator John Oswald: "I can remember seeing a pair of eyes staring at me and saying, 'Don't be afraid' [not audibly, but in her head]. I covered my eyes and yanked the wheel. I was petrified."[16]

The Sergeant Moody case also contained this peculiarity. He described this mode of communication with the aliens as being almost as if you are thinking something in your own head.

The classic Barney and Betty Hill abduction case of September 19, 1961, near Woodstock, New Hampshire, also involved this type of communication.[17] Barney reported that the UFO's occupants spoke to him by mental telepathy from the hovering object: "He's just telling me, 'don't be afraid.'" Later, when the craft reportedly landed and the entities approached their car, he reported: "the eyes are talking to me... telling me, 'don't be afraid.'" Betty also stated that she "knew what they were thinking."

This phenomenon was also an integral part of the already cited Lehi, Utah, case. One of the witnesses described the small entities as having "thought at me with their heads."

Interestingly enough, some pertinent remarks about this type of communication were discussed at a Military Electronics Conference on Communication with Extraterrestrial Intelligence held from September 22 to 24, 1965, in Washington, D.C. One of the panel members, Dr.

William O. Davis, director of research at Huyck Corporation (Stamford, Connecticut), stated the following concerning this fascinating subject:

How do we communicate? Well, we have talked about the linguistic approach. We have talked about Dr. Lilly's approach with nonhuman forms. I think I would like to break the problem down a little more.

There are really three different cases we should worry about. *First* of all is an encounter with a lower order of intelligence than our own. This would be the case if we should land on a planet and find it occupied with life at the level of bees or cows and presumably nonintelligent, or at least not yet at our level. In this particular case, I think that the best we could hope for would be the type of communication we establish with dogs and horses, a symbiosis or—and this is disputable—a telepathic rapport with them. It would be unlikely that we could establish communication at the verbal level or at the level of symbology.

The *second* case is where we find people of precisely equal evolution. Now, this is very improbable.... Even 15 years in our history would make a tremendous difference, either backwards or forwards. If you look at the technological trend curves, for example, you find that by the year 2000 everything is asymptotic, and it is extremely likely that technological revolution per se will have played itself out by that time. Other trends indicate that from here on, increasing emphasis is going to be on understanding the mind and how it operates. Some of the work that Dr. Puharich has done is a little controversial, too, such as studying extrasensory perception with people having extreme talents, which indicates that there are relationships between these ESP talents and other natural phenomena, and indicates that as we go on we may be able to learn how to improve our ability to communicate, at least at the symbolic level, by ESP means. Certainly even today we do a great deal, I suspect, of our communication at the emotional level by extrasensory means.

If we were to encounter somebody of equal intelligence, I think we would have a problem. We would undoubtedly fight them. This, to my way of thinking, is the least probable and the most dangerous of the three cases.

The *third* case is that the *most probable encounter* is with a *higher* form of life, or at least a more advanced form, because these beings would be more likely to reach us first than vice versa. If we assume that they understand more about the mind than we do— and let's say they understand more about ESP or it turns out to be a human-type phenomenon—they should be able to detect us. After all, we know all kinds of fields associated with the physical world, the world of entropy. It is not illogical to assume that life may have as yet undetected fields and radiation associated with it. They wouldn't have to scour the whole universe for us. They would simply focus their life-detecting device. The nice thing about this hypothetical contact is that communication would be their problem. We wouldn't have to worry about it. They would come to us. As a matter of fact, I strongly suspect that the first communication is very likely to be telepathic.[18]

9. The general configuration of the craft and noises associated with it

Sergeant Moody also described an *elevator* in the craft he was taken into, noting that the floor seemed to give way like an elevator. One of the remarkable internal consistencies of this particular case concerned Betty's detailed drawings of things she had witnessed during the reported experience. The amount of detail in these drawings appeared to have been in direct proportion to the length of observing time Betty was allowed during the alleged abduction.

Investigator Fred Youngren performed a fascinating analysis of Betty's sketches of the UFO's interior. Fred has a master's degree in aerospace engineering and holds a managerial position within the defense industry. He obtained estimated dimensions of various segments of the object from Betty, then combined her drawings and narrative data to produce a feasible floor plan of the UFO.[19]

10. The physical examination

There are a number of similarities between the physical examination administered to Betty Andreasson and those allegedly given to other abductees. Sergeant Moody, for example, states that he woke up lying on a metallic table—a solid block sitting on the floor. He looked up and saw one of the small creatures standing beside him. His first impulse was to jump up and hit it, but he found that he was being totally restrained by an unseen force.

11. The laying on of hands to relieve pain

Betty Hill also reported being probed by long needles, including one that was inserted into her navel for a *pregnancy* test. When she screamed out in pain, the leader of the entities came over, put his hands in front of her eyes, and said that it would be all right and that she wouldn't feel it.

12. The eyelike lens in the examining room

The eyelike lens mentioned by Betty seems to have its counterpart in other cases. On October 11, 1973, Charles Hickson and Calvin Parker reported that two creatures had floated from a hovering craft and grabbed them off a pier at Pascagoula, Mississippi. The creatures floated them into the craft, where Hickson claimed to have been examined by a device that reminded him of a big eye. Betty Hill also described a device that the aliens used to examine her as being like a microscope with a big lens.

13. The immersion of Betty's body in a fluid during transit

The Brazilian newspaper *0 Dia,* of April 22, 1976, mentions a Mario Restier, who reported that he had been abducted by three creatures from a disc-shaped object who communicated with him by telepathic means. After being taken aboard the craft, he claims the aliens ordered him to get into a *glass box filled with liquid.* They explained to him that this was the only method by which the human body could be protected against the effects of their form of travel. Perhaps the immersion chair that Betty was placed in was for this very same purpose. Could it be possible that this strange chair was in reality a liquid-filled high-g acceleration chamber to protect her from the high acceleration involved during the trip to the alien place?

Betty had the distinct impression that while her body was immersed in one of the tanklike seats, the oval craft brought her to an alien place. It is possible that the seat was designed to protect humans from the effects of acceleration and speed beyond our comprehension. Liquid would cushion the pressures by distributing stresses evenly over Betty's body. (Water is also used in nuclear plants as a shield against radiation—which is also known to exist in earth's Van Allen belts.) Lastly, the syrup fed to Betty through a tube seems to have been some form of tranquilizer that made her "feel good."

Looking back on the incident, it would seem that Betty experienced the same weightlessness that our own astronauts did. She seems to have been artificially held down, except when the aliens floated her at will from one position to another. The heavy feeling that she felt while on the UFO may have been an induced localized gravitational force that counteracted the weightlessness—or a byproduct of extreme acceleration. A similar applied force probably kept her upright on the black track transportation system.

Even the small globes carried by the aliens may not be entirely unprecedented in the annals of UFO history. Early in 1967, NICAP received a startling report from a gentleman who refused to give his name and address. Although this case could not be properly investigated, it nonetheless bears a striking similarity to this aspect of the Andreasson Affair.

On the evening of February 5, 1967 (interestingly enough, only 11 days after Betty's experience), a young man in Hilliard, Ohio, said he heard a "strange noise" and a dog barking. Looking up, he saw a UFO 75 feet long and about 75 feet high come in low over a road shoulder. The object, he said, landed on three legs in a field, and "beings" emerged. They were carrying *small circular balls,* which they placed on the ground around the sides of the ship. Then the witness stepped on a twig that snapped, which immediately caught the attention of the "beings." Their leader ran after the observer who, badly frightened, attempted to run. However, the creature caught him by the back of the neck, immediately leaving a burned wound that, according to the witness, was later confirmed by unnamed Air Force officers investigating the incident. He said still another of the creatures approached, and both dragged him back to the saucer. As they got almost to the door of the craft, the humanoids looked at each other as if panic-stricken. They dropped the scared witness, gathered up the balls, and took off in the UFO.[20]

Thus, there are a number of interesting parallels between the Andreasson Affair and other CE-IV reports on record. There seem to be too many such similarities, cast in a logical structure within her account, to dismiss them all as products of cryptoamnesia, a term that refers to the mind's ability to record and subconsciously store all sorts of data from daily experience. Information culled from books, magazines, newspapers, radio, TV, recordings, and conversations all contributes to our subconscious memory bank.

This, of course, could include data on other UFO cases. In fact, Betty admitted having read books and articles on UFOs following her 1967 experience, and her initial letter to Dr. Hynek reflected theories and ideas obviously gleaned from a reading of uncritical UFO literature. Yet some of the subtle details she related—though *extremely* uncommon—*do* correlate with other unpublished UFO cases we have investigated. (These particular characteristics must remain confidential so as not to compromise our investigations into future cases.)

How could Betty's subconscious have "remembered" details from cases that have not yet been printed? If we grant that *some* other reported UFO experiences are grounded in reality, these common and not-so-common characteristics of *other* UFO reports add support for the authenticity of Betty Andreasson's report. I personally found it very hard not to accept that the Andreasson family had a bona fide UFO experience.

In retrospect, the Andreasson Affair can be divided into five segments:

Segment 1: The flashing lights and power failure were experienced and consciously remembered by Betty and Becky Andreasson, and Waino and Eva Aho. The younger children did not remember anything.

Segment 2: Alien entities were observed by Betty and Becky Andreasson, and Waino Aho.

Segment 3: Betty alone experienced the UFO episode.

Segment 4: Betty alone experienced a visit to an alien realm.

Segment 5: Betty alone experienced the return to her home.

Because segments 1 and 2 were witnessed by more than one person, they logically receive higher credibility ratings than segments 3 through 5, which essentially involved Betty alone.

The controversial segment 4, during which Betty saw the huge bird, presented the greatest dilemma to the field investigators, the hypnotist, and the psychiatrist. Where *was* Betty taken? Were the red and green areas part of an underground colony on earth, on the moon, or on one of our neighboring planets? Was the alien colony located within a hollowed-out asteroid, or did Betty visit a vast artificial mother ship? Did Betty leave our solar system entirely, via an acceleration and technology entirely beyond our ken? These and many other questions remain unanswered. And because of its uniqueness within UFO literature and its strong religious overtones, the Phoenix episode was difficult to accept as a *physical* experience.

Segment 4 seemed just as real to Betty as the other segments, but because of the high degree of strangeness associated with it, one does tend to want to disassociate it from the rest of the report. Regarding the bird and the voice, our attitudes varied: This segment was a nonrelated vision instigated by Betty's own religious beliefs; this episode was a programmed vision induced by the entities; it could have been a staged, symbolic (yet physical) initiation rite as described by Betty; it was a deliberate deception on the part of the aliens to make human beings believe in a UFO/religion connection. And lastly, perhaps there was a possible link between UFOs and religion. In any case, the Phoenix episode remains a puzzle.

If taken at face value, however, the other segments of the Andreasson Affair are incredible enough, in both their content and their implications. If we accept Betty and Becky's account as true, then an actual alien craft landed or appeared in the Andreassons' backyard. The strange craft contained aliens of unknown origin. Their paranormal powers indicate that no one is exempt from a CE-IV.

It is especially unnerving to realize that the glasslike chairs in the half-cylinder room were shaped to the stature of a *human* body. The tubes connected to Betty's nostrils and mouth were designed for air-breathing persons. The entire operation seems to have been tailored for human beings!

Indeed, according to Quazgaa, Betty is just one of many persons who have undergone such an experience. And before bringing this comparative analysis to an end, we must turn to one of the most striking similarities discovered during our investigation of the Andreasson Affair. It has to do with the needle and possibly implanted BB-like object in Betty's nose.

C·H·A·P·T·E·R 12

➤ Hints of an Earlier Encounter ➤

Other cases seem to have parallels to Betty's experience of having a needle inserted into her nose—for example, the Lehi, Utah, case mentioned earlier. When Aerial Phenomena Research Organization (APRO) hypnosis consultant Dr. Harder asked the abductee, "Where was the needle?" she replied, "I could see it coming toward me...to the front of me." Dr. Harder tried unsuccessfully to break through an apparent mental block instilled by the entities that prevented any further details about the needles. APRO consultant Dr. Leo Sprinkle was more successful concerning a case at Fargo, North Dakota. Under hypnosis, the abductee, Mrs. Sandra Larson, described a portion of the physical examination administered to her by the aliens: "It was like somebody took a knife and made the inside of my nose sore." Because her eyes were closed during the examination, she could describe only what she was feeling. When asked to describe the instrument being used, she continued by saying that it felt like a "little knife" placed in her nose.[1]

One of our most provocative questions concerns the BB-like object at the end of the needlelike probe that was apparently *removed* from Betty's nose. How did it get there? What was its purpose? The answer to this puzzle may very well be connected with the following case. It is of high significance for comparison purposes, because it has not been published outside of a certain circle of investigators who specialize in the study of UFO occupant reports.

To the best of my knowledge, it is the only other report on record describing this particular procedure. The following is quoted from the investigators' report on this fascinating case. (The witnesses' and investigators' names are on file, but must be kept confidential at this time.)

Witness: And they released this little tiny thing, like a buckshot.

Investigator: What did they release it from?

Witness: From the needle.

Investigator: What was the needle like?

Witness: It was sort of like a long needle that was sticking in my side.

Investigator: Was it a hollow needle, and then ejected through the hollow needle, or attached to the—

Witness: I didn't see the needle [*i.e., when the tiny device was released*]. They had my arm up over my head, like that, so I couldn't see what they were doing here. And then they said, "I hope your body doesn't reject it. With this implant we're putting in there is going to come better communications and power, and we hope your body doesn't reject it. If it doesn't reject it, we'll activate it in, uh, three or four weeks." And then they turned me over on my back and said, "Now you're going to sleep."

Was this object Betty described, then, an implant? And how did it get there in the first place? The answer seems couched in an astounding revelation by Betty during our last hypnotic session.

At one time, Betty's captors had mentioned to her where they had come from. But Betty couldn't pronounce it. We attempted to obtain the phonetic pronunciation of their place of origin.

Fred: In one of the previous sessions, you told us a little bit about a place where the beings came from. You had trouble spelling or saying it. Would you try once again to recall that?

Betty: It's a Z...[*Pause*] some S's and a P in it.

Fred: Are there more than four letters in that?

Betty: There's a lot more than that, yes.

Fred: Do you recall it well enough to spell the whole word?

Betty: I don't know. They talk it funny.

Fred: Can you say it the way they talk it?

Betty: No.

Fred: Mimic it?

Betty: Uh, mimic it. Let's see—um...[*Attempts to pronounce it without success, sighs*] I can't do it.

Fred: All right. Where did you get the information?

Betty: He told me it.

Fred: Who told you?

Betty: The beings told me it.

Fred: Do you know which one told you?

Betty: [*Sighs*] There are so many of them.

Fred: Was it one that you've told us about?

Betty: No.

Fred: Then when did you get the information?

Betty: When I was there.

Fred: When you were *there?*

Betty: Yes.

Fred: How long ago was that?

Betty: A long time ago.

Betty's answer caused quite a stir in the room. It came as a complete surprise, although we should have expected it when she had described the removal of the object through her nose.

Fred: You mean in 1967? Is that when you got the information? [*25-second pause*] Was it before 1967, Betty?

Betty: Yes.

Jules: It was! Do you remember how long before 1967? [*25-second pause*] Can you tell us any more about it? Maybe you can't remember the date, but can you tell us any more about that?

Betty: No.

Fred: How do you know that that is the place where the beings come from?

Betty: That is where they come from.

Fred: I didn't hear you. Did you say that *is* where they come from?

Betty: Yes.

Fred: Why do you—how do you know that? Why do you know that is where they come from? Because they told you?

Betty: Yes, they told me. *And I was there.*

Joseph: You went to the place where they came from?

Betty: Yes.

Joseph: Did you see other ships still there?

Betty: Yes, there's other ships there. They live in a gray atmosphere, hazy all the time.

Fred: Can you recall anything about the occasion?

Betty: Seems very gray and dark.

Fred: How old were you at the time that this happened?

At that point Betty became very upset.

Jules: What are you upset about, Betty?

Betty: I don't like this place. It's so dark and gray.

Joseph: Which place? Are you back there now?

Betty: Yes.

Fred: You don't know how old you are?

Betty: No.

Fred: Was it before 1967?

Betty: Yes.

Joseph: Are you frightened of the place?

Betty: Yes.

Fred: Would you like to leave that place?

Betty: Yes.

When we tried to bring her back to relive what appeared to have been a pre-1967 UFO abduction experience, Betty became literally terrified. Harold strongly suggested that we should not inquire further because it upset Betty too much.

A prior UFO experience would solve several puzzling aspects in this case. First, in an earlier session, Betty inadvertently gave us information that could not have been obtained during the 1967 abduction. It hinted of an earlier incident.

Ray: Betty, you indicate that the ship was sectioned off and had different levels. Somehow the lower section whirled, and the top section remained stationary. At times the top also moved— especially when there was to be a change in direction. What confuses me is, at what point during your experience did you actually see something like this? As far as I can remember, you have never seen the object in flight or at a distance.

Betty: I really don't know, Ray, when I saw it. But I know it.

Moreover, psychic phenomena have played a part in the lives of many who have had a Close Encounter UFO experience. And the Andreasson family was no exception. Several months after her harrowing UFO experience of January 1967, Betty stood at the sink doing dishes. Abruptly and without warning, something took control of her mind.

Betty: It was as if the infinite opened up to me. And it scared me to death, because I was seeing inventions so far advanced— thousands of years advanced—and yet it seemed just a pinpoint or scratch in the infinite. I was afraid 'cause it wasn't me controlling it. It was something else. As soon as I became fearful, it shut off.

For several years after the incident, Betty received similar flashes of insight, some of which may have been connected with her UFO experience. One of these involved a being of light in her home: "I was lying there, and I turned my head toward my husband, who was asleep. And then, I heard noises like somebody opening and closing drawers. I turned my head to the direction and I saw this 'light-being.' This was a bright, illuminated being about four to five feet tall. It wasn't fat or slim. It was just right. The hands were there, the arms, the legs, and the head, but it had no features. It was just all light. It leaped down the stairs."

One night in 1975, Becky had an experience of her own. As Betty tells it: "The upstairs kitchen of our house was not as yet finished. Only the bedrooms were finished which we were using. We were cooking and eating in the cellar kitchen until the new one was ready. Becky had been awakened by her new baby in the early morning hours and had gone to the cellar apartment to heat the baby's bottle on the gas stove. Before going down to the cellar, she flicked on all the lights. Suddenly all the lights went out and huge glowing eyes peered at her from the cellar window. She screamed and ran upstairs, leaving the gas burning. There was a power failure that night *only* in our area. We learned the next day that the lights had come on by themselves, and the power company did not know what had caused the failure just in our area."

Hallucination? Imagination? Paranormal phenomena? Who can tell for sure? Prior to the UFO encounter recalled under hypnosis, the Andreasson family had considered these odd but still isolated events. Now they took on a new meaning, as did the several strange events that occurred when Betty lived at Westminster, Massachusetts, way *before* the 1967 UFO encounter.

One evening in the mid-1950s, when Betty was very young, she was lying in bed. Suddenly she had a feeling that someone was staring at her through a second-story window. She was so fearful that she couldn't force herself to look at the window. On the following morning, she noticed that small trees near the window were bent over.

On an evening during the early 1960s, Betty had another strange experience. She was reading her Bible on the sofa when again she had the same strong feeling of being watched. Looking up slowly, she was startled to see a face staring at her through the window. The figure had red hair, red eyebrows, and black, piercing eyes. His gaze was fixed and appeared malevolent. She forced her eyes away from his hypnotic expression and looked back down at her Bible. Then she slowly got up and left the room before running to the front door and shouting to her father for help. (Her parents lived next door.) When her father arrived, the Peeping Tom had vanished. Betty said he looked like a normal person except for the penetrating black eyes.

The final incident in Westminster—the only one recalled when something akin to a UFO was involved—occurred when Becky was about 8 years old, which would place it around 1964. One night Becky woke up to see a glowing yellow-orange ball hovering outside her bedroom window. The object had directed a narrow beam of light at her. Becky's screams of terror caused Betty to rush upstairs to her aid, but by the time she arrived, the strange phenomenon had disappeared. Shortly after this, Becky developed the uncanny ability to automatically write page after page of strange symbols. The strange script was found to be very similar to the so-called spirit writing practiced by the Shakers, an early American religious sect.

Strange incidents also occurred after the family moved to South Ashburnham. Whether or not they were connected with an *earlier* UFO abduction must remain in the realm of speculation. But the fact remains that a pre-1967 abduction would explain why the entities registered surprise at Betty's having "parts missing," the result of the 1965 hysterectomy. It would also explain the presence of the tiny object in Betty's head. It is interesting to note that the entities made a puzzling statement just prior to its removal: They told Betty that they were *awakening* something. Perhaps this bristled object was a highly sophisticated monitoring device emplaced within her during an earlier abduction!

This theory brings to mind some experiments that man is conducting with lower life forms here on earth. We go to great lengths to study habits, environment, and idiosyncracies. Consider the following analogy:

A black bear is out rummaging for food in a heavily wooded area that he shares with a goodly number of other wild creatures. Sniffing the air cautiously, he cuts across a large field on the way to a river to fish for salmon. Suddenly, a foreign noise coming from above causes him to look up. Terrified, he sees a strange, noisy, whirring, birdlike thing hovering directly above him. He starts to run back to the woods with the huge "bird" in hot pursuit. Suddenly, a sharp, brief pain stabs into his side. He continues to run, but an inexplicable feeling of drowsiness overwhelms him. The bear slumps to the ground in a sound sleep.

The "bird" lands. It is a helicopter, and out of it step several scientists. One still holds the rifle that has just fired a tranquilizer-filled dart into the fleeing bear. Carefully, a wildlife biologist tags the bear and places a radio transmitter collar and temperature probe about the sleeping bear's neck. The scientists then board the helicopter and depart.

Later, the bear stirs. Perhaps vague images of the frightening chase still linger in his mind. Most likely they are dismissed as a bad dream brought on by eating decayed rabbit meat earlier that morning. He is hungry. So he lumbers off to the river, where there are fat, migrating salmon just waiting to be caught.

Seven hundred miles above him, a highly sophisticated satellite dubbed *Nimbus* wheels around the planet in a predetermined course. It signals the radio transmitter attached to the bear. It, in turn, begins to transmit data gathered by special sensors. *Nimbus* then re-transmits the signals to a ground radio station in Fairbanks, Alaska.[2] Then the data is sent to Goddard Space Flight Center at Maryland, where it emerges as a computer readout.

Meanwhile, the bear continues to fish, hunt, sleep, and hibernate. He remains completely oblivious to the fact that his bodily functions and exact whereabouts are being monitored by a super-intelligent species— man. How could a bear even begin to comprehend such a thing? Similarly, how could a human even begin to understand how a super-intelligent race might similarly monitor man's doings? Could it be that the little BB-shaped object that the entities were "awakening" was a monitoring device?

The entities knew where to find Betty at Ashburnham. They knew her name and told her that they had known all of the trouble she had been going through. This could be ascribed to the "mind reading" aspect of telepathy, except that the entities seemed *surprised* to find "parts missing"— evidently the result of Betty's hysterectomy, which would, of course, have taken place *after* Betty's first abduction.

This also brings to mind a statement made by an alien to Betty Hill, another abductee, back in 1961. In the book *The Interrupted Journey,* Betty Hill is quoted in a conversation with her alien captor:

But there are other people in this country who...would be most happy to talk with him, and they could answer all his questions. And, maybe if he could come back, all his questions would have answers. But if I did, I wouldn't know where to meet him. And he [the alien] said, "Don't worry. If we decide to come back, we will be able to find you, all right. We always find those we want to."[3]

Perhaps even now, individuals like Betty Hill and Betty Andreasson are being monitored by instruments far out in space. In any case, succeeding events were to prove that the entities *were* keeping a most unsettlingly close check on Betty's activities.

E·P·I·L·O·G·U·E

➤ A New Investigation ≺

So long ago and still my initial investigation into the abduction experience of Betty Andreasson in 1967 remains fresh in my mind. At that time in 1977, I was 42 years of age. Now, at the age of 80, I find myself writing an epilogue to yet another edition of *The Andreasson Affair.* So where do I begin? The best place would be where the book left off with Betty's 1967 experience with the Phoenix. At that time she was told in no uncertain terms that she had been chosen to tell the world about the alien entities that had abducted her. How has this come to pass since that terrifying encounter? Let us see.

Her experiences were first revealed in the original publication of *The Andreasson Affair* by Prentice-Hall in 1979, which made the *New York Times* Best-Seller List. Soon after that the book was reprinted by Bantam in 1980 and again in 1988. Bantam sponsored a two-week nation-wide book tour during which Betty and I appeared on radio and TV throughout the United States. *The Andreasson Affair* was reprinted in several foreign countries and movie rights were purchased by Universal Studios, which still holds the rights.

This certainly was a good start to informing the public about her experiences, but it did not end there. The information obtained from the original investigation documented in this book was just the tip of the proverbial iceberg of Betty's startling experiences revealed during my follow-on 17-year investigation into the UFO and paranormal experiences of Betty and her family. These were documented in my four follow-on books that were published between 1982 and 1995. Now here we are again with yet another reprint of *The Andreasson Affair* and also the beginning of negotiations with Universal Studios to obtain the rights for a movie. So much, so far, for Betty's experiences being made known to the world. The rest of this epilogue is a summary of what Betty and her family have gone through since her 1967 experience. It will be divided into four sections that encompass the four phases of my overall investigation of Betty's and Bob Luca's families.

Phase I

After Betty's divorce, she temporarily moved to Pompano Beach, Florida, in the fall of 1977, where she purchased a small house at Pompano Beach and took a job at the Clock restaurant as a waitress. Betty's abrupt decision to go to Florida ended my Phase I investigation and I decided to write a book about Betty's experiences, which culminated in *The Andreasson Affair.*

Phase II

Betty met Bob Luca while working at the Clock restaurant. Their meeting was highly synchronistic. Bob, like Betty, had a UFO experience in 1967 with a period of missing time. Betty told him about our investigation and he decided to undergo an investigation to probe his missing time experience. During the investigation, Betty married Bob in 1978 and moved into a house in Meriden, Connecticut.

In the meantime I spent most of 1978 writing *The Andreasson Affair,* keeping track of Betty by occasional letters and phone calls. Betty temporarily moved back to Ashburnham, Massachusetts, in the fall of 1978 to sell her house. During that time she told me about a number of strange things that happened in the house: poltergeist phenomena, unexplained noises and voices, and small floating balls of light. I was curious about how a small object had been removed from Betty's nose during her 1967 abduction and about her mentioning a "big door" by the aliens. Also, I was most interested in looking into Bob's UFO/missing time experience. A team of investigators was again put together and the new Phase II investigation was launched. Both Betty and Bob underwent 13 audio-taped hypnosis sessions.

We started with Bob first on March 17 and 24, 1980. When asked under hypnosis to describe his first UFO experience, we expected to hear about his missing time experience. Instead Bob described in a childlike manner, a UFO experience as a 5-year-old in 1944. At that time he was living with his grandmother in Meriden, Connecticut. While playing on a swing placed in a field behind the house, a disk-shaped object suddenly appeared. Two small, gray entities could be seen in a clear dome on top. A beam of light from the object hit and paralyzed Bob. A message was given to him telepathically. A brief excerpt follows:

> They're telling me things. Telling something, be good when I am older.... I can't say that yet.... They visit other people, and, ah, they're going to visit other people too.... Prepare us something good. Going to be for mankind.... In time *people* in the *light* will be back and the people that have seen them before will not be afraid when they come back.

Again, under hypnosis, Bob recalled his adult UFO sighting in 1967 while driving to a beach in Connecticut. On the way he noticed workers at a railroad track looking up at the sky. He stopped the car and got out to look. He saw two silver, wingless cigar-shaped objects. Each released a smaller disk-shaped object, which flew off in different directions. Amazed at what he saw, he then continued on to the beach.

On the way to the beach, he was shocked to see a domed disk-shaped object appear and approach the car in a falling leaf motion. A red beam from the object hit Bob and he found himself with a small gray entity entering the craft. He was made to undress and was placed upon a table where he was examined by several other aliens. They looked identical to the type Betty had encountered in 1967 except they were dressed in red rather than blue tight-fitting suits. The next thing he remembered was being back in the car driving to the beach and arriving two hours later than planned.

On the following day, March 25, 1980, Betty was placed under hypnosis. She also relived a UFO experience at age 7, at Leominster, Massachusetts, in 1944. While in a playhouse waiting for her girlfriend, a bright marble-shaped object flew in and affixed itself to Betty's temple. She felt faint and fell back as she heard a voice in her head. She was told:

> *They have been watching me.... I'm coming along fine...good progress.... I was going to be happy very soon.... Other people were going to be happy.... Getting some things ready to show me.... It wouldn't be until I would be 12.*

During several hypnosis sessions in April 1980, Betty was regressed to age 12. At that time Betty was living in Westminster, Massachusetts. While walking in the woods she encountered a small gray alien in a strange suit. A glowing ball was released from an orifice on the suit. It affixed itself to her temple and a voice was heard that stated:

> *She's got another year.... They are preparing things for her to see...that it may help people in the future.*

Our team found this fascinating. It seems that aliens were waiting for Betty to mature sexually. Also was the fact that both Betty and Bob had been abducted as children in 1944 and as adults in 1967. We wondered if Bob's abrupt decision to travel to Florida may have been controlled by the aliens.

Strange events experienced by Betty's family occurred all throughout my investigation over the years: men dressed in black clothes observing her house and black unmarked helicopters flying over her home and car. (One even hovered directly above her as she worked in her garden.) Such strange things even occurred during one of our hypnosis sessions. Betty saw an alien appear and fade out in the room during the April 21, 1980 session. Then a ball of light the size of a dime appeared in the room. It was witnessed by one of our investigating team members, a lieutenant in the police force.

The glowing ball was resting on a curtain as if observing the session. He sat for a few minutes trying to figure out its source. He first thought it to have been an outside light shining through a window behind the curtain. He got up to investigate and as he did the light blinked out. When he pulled the curtain back, there just was a blank wall! During this session and follow-on sessions in May, Betty was regressed to age 13 and relived experiences that rivaled the tale of the *Wizard of Oz*. A summary follows.

Betty had gotten up early in the morning for a walk through the woods to Crocker Pond. As she climbed some stairs to a field she saw what looked like a moon in the sky moving toward her. Suddenly she found herself in a craft with the typical gray entities who told her that they would bring her home to see "The One." This indeed did occur and will be summarized, but first, what else happened?

Betty was examined by aliens in a number of strange ways. She experienced some remarkable sights including being taken through a glass-like forest with trees and life-forms composed of clear crystal. When she touched a butterfly it came to life momentarily before becoming a tiny ball of light and returning to its crystal form. She was put aboard a craft. The aliens placed a device that kept her tongue clamped down. Then she was placed on a round, cushion-like bed where she felt herself being pressed down. The craft flew to an icy installation reached by an underwater journey. After disembarking from the craft, Betty and the alien entities walked through an icy corridor. They passed what appeared to be rows and rows of upright clear-faced cubicles containing what appeared to be mummified people from different times and cultures—literally *a museum of time!*

To visit "The One" she was made to lie in a coffin-like device, which transported her to a place that had a huge glass door. She found herself coming out of her body and confronted by tall blue-eyed human-like entities and a small gray entity. Betty was commanded to enter the Great Door. She did and experienced someone or something or both that she was not able to describe because of its beauty and secrecy imposed upon her. It seemed to be identical to what is called a near-death experience.

The hypnotist tried every way he knew to extract what Betty had seen during the Great Door experience but to no avail. A summary of what he could extract follows:

1. Everybody is nice. They are just growing.
2. Everything fits together. Everything is one.
3. Those without love have nothing.
4. Love is the answer to all things.

The best description that Betty would give to us of what lay behind the Great Door was: "It is the entrance into the other world. The world where light is."

After the Great Door experience, Betty again was placed back in the same device. It transported her back to where she had been previously. There, she was examined again. This included her being placed before a TV-like monitor where she observed balls of light and symbols, having her spinal fluid tapped, and a very traumatic operation that removed her eye. After it was removed, a tiny implant was placed behind it. (An implant was taken from Betty's nose during her 1967 abduction experience.) Betty was then flown by a strange craft, with tubes mounted on its top, which landed near Crocker Pond, where she had set out for that morning. She was placed beside the pond and made to forget what had happened to her. When Betty came to, she thought that she had walked to the pond as planned.

The last hypnosis sessions of our Phase II investigation took place on May 29 and June 11, 1980. During the session, Betty relived an experience at age 24 that took place at Westminster, Massachusetts. She was drawn by a strange force that led her to leave her house and walk up to some woods. In the woods she was confronted by a tall gray entity that telepathically spoke the following message to her:

1. I am not to fear. The Lord is with me.

2. I am going to go through many things. Love will show me the answers.

3. Many things will be revealed to me. I shall grow naturally.

4. My faith in the light will bring many others to the light.

5. For every place there is an existence. Everything has been formed to unite.

6. To keep my faith for the Lord Jesus is with me.

7. I shall understand as time goes by and not to be anxious.

Our plans to continue hypnosis were dashed. Every attempt to do so caused Betty to experience pain when asked to relive her next experience.

The Phase II investigation came to an abrupt halt. I wrote up a 477-page report of our findings and another book entitled *The Andreasson Affair— Phase Two.*[1]

I continued off and on to have contact with the Lucas but was disappointed not to probe their experiences further because many of them matched phenomena experienced by myself and my family. These also included UFO abductions and all sorts of paranormal phenomena. Later I compared them in my book entitled *The Andreasson Legacy.*[2] However, this was to occur years away.

Meanwhile Betty and Bob went through a difficult phase of adjustment. They shunned public discussion about their encounters with UFOs. They became modern-day nomads. They sold and moved from one house to another, perhaps trying to escape a host of paranormal phenomena that plagued them. These included more periods of missing time, out-of-body experiences (OBEs), and sightings of UFOS. I carefully monitored these events and periodically asked if they would like to continue an investigation using hypnosis, but this was always rejected.

Later, much to my surprise, Betty and Bob decided to talk publicly about their experiences. They solicited media interviews and Betty made papier-mâché models of the alien beings. She began painting very realistic scenes from her experiences. Soon after, the break to the deadlocked investigation came about in a totally unexpected manner. It began with a troubled phone call from Betty in 1987.

Betty said that she was experiencing flashbacks and dreams of a woman's face. The eyes of the woman literally cried out for help. The contorted face haunted her so much that she felt compelled to undergo hypnosis to discover the woman's identity. I agreed to help and initiated a Phase III investigation into the ongoing Andreasson Affair.

Phase III

New hypnosis sessions were conducted on January 23, February 7, and February 10, 1988. These sessions were the most important carried out during my investigations because they revealed *why* the aliens were abducting people.

Amazingly, Betty underwent hypnosis easily without pain when asked to describe her next UFO encounter. Her memory moved to the year 1973, during which she and her husband, Jim, lived in their new home in Ashburnham, Massachusetts. She relived awaking in bed to a bright light that shone through the windows. She attempted without success to wake Jim. The light seemed strange. Frightened, she crawled under her covers with one arm hanging out. Then, something grabbed her arm and pulled off the covers. She looked up to see four gray aliens standing around the bed. Jim seemed to be in a state of suspended animation and was unaware of what was happening.

The gray entities took Betty out to the field near her house. A craft hovered above and shone a light upon them. It beamed them up into the craft, where Betty was placed upon some kind of a chair. She suddenly felt heavy and squished as if experiencing strong G-forces. She felt sick. An entity placed something in her ear and she felt better. She was removed from the chair and brought into a room where aliens were standing around a woman lying on a table. The following are brief excerpts from the hypnosis sessions.

> *There's a lady lying on a table over there. And they're bringing me toward that person and she's looking at me. She looks so-o-o-o-o afraid. She looks like she's crying out for help to me. And I feel I can move my hands and everything up to my waist. But the bottom part of me is like, like stone. That poor lady. She seems so afraid. And I'm calming her down.*

Betty recognized the woman's face. It was the woman of her dreams and flashbacks. It was made known that she was there to comfort the woman while the aliens were operating on her. Betty watched one of the aliens place his hand on the woman's head. She seemed to go to sleep.

> *They're taking something from her. Looks like a fetus.* [Betty was visibly shaken and became terrified.]

Two fetuses were removed. Their eyelids were quickly circumcised. One fetus had normal white eyes but the other had big black eyes like the alien entities. The one with the white eyes was placed in a bin of liquid. The one with the black eyes was placed in a strange tank filled with liquid, which was attached to a cylindrical thing. Needles were placed in the soft spot of its head and in the ears. Betty was terribly upset with witnessing such a thing and asked why they were doing it.

And they're telling me that they're doing this because the human race will become sterile by the pollution and the bacteria and the terrible things that are on the earth. They're telling me that they have to extrapolate and put their protoplasma in the nucleus of the fetus and the paragenetic. [Betty stops and sounds completely frustrated.] I don't understand them. Something like the paragenetic will utilize the tissue and nutrients to—I don't know—transfer the creature or something like that.... They said they're Watchers...and they keep seed from man and woman so the human will not be lost.... Man is going to become sterile.... They are the same substance as Man.... The fetuses become them.

Who could ever have imaged such things? Their very improbability adds to the probability of their truth especially when hundreds of other abducted females report fetuses being taken from them. They also report seeing fetuses being kept in artificial womb-like tanks. If we take their reports at face value, they provide logical answers to the key question of the UFO phenomenon. In other words, they fit the missing piece of the puzzle.

Betty and the woman were made to strip and take a shower of a substance that would protect them from static electricity when the craft landed to take in water from a lake. At the lake another craft landed and Betty saw a naked man in a *floating-walking movement* taken from it. After the water extraction, Betty was taken aboard the craft again. While on board she was brought to a huge biosphere that housed tiny alien entities. Some had eyes like humans and others had large black eyes like Betty's captors. She was then returned to her home at Ashburnham and, as usual, was programmed to forget her experience. The hypnosis sessions continued between February and July 1989. A summary of Betty's experiences follows.

Several bedroom encounters took place between 1975 and 1977. At age 38, an alien appeared and told her that it was time to remember her experiences. At age 39, one of the strange entities again appeared by her bedside and told her that marital difficulties would end but that there would be hardship. This, of course, happened when her husband left her with the house and outstanding bills to pay.

At age 40, a gray alien awoke her and told her of the impending death of her two sons and that they could not interfere to save them. Betty did not remember this consciously until it was revealed through hypnosis. However, the day before her sons were killed in an automobile accident, she phoned to tell me that she had a premonition that something terrible was going to happen. She was in tears and asked if she could travel from her home in Connecticut to where I lived in Wenham, Massachusetts, to talk about it. When she and Bob arrived, I did the best I could to calm her fears before they left for home. The next day her sons had their fatal accident.

In 1978, Betty and Bob heard a whirring sound above their house. Concurrently, both were lifted out of their bodies and, along with others, entered a huge round amphitheater-like enclosure. They were greeted by tall, robed human-looking entities. They found themselves on a high walkway that surrounded the enclosure. Bob was separated from Betty. He was told that he was not as spiritually advanced as Betty and was held to wait for her. During that time he received answers to many questions that he asked an alien who guarded him. Betty, on the other hand, was allowed to participate with a number of light beings in a fantastic procedure that changed her and them into *balls of light* and back to their *light-being* form.

During this abduction, Betty glanced down to the floor below and gasped. She saw two daughters and Bob's daughter on tables being examined by aliens. She was so troubled by what she saw that the hypnotist had her temporarily forget what she saw. They were returned to their bodies and had no idea of what had just happened to them.

The hypnosis sessions continued. In 1981 and 1982, strange figures were seen momentarily in their bedroom at night. In 1984, Betty saw shadowy figures in her kitchen while watching TV. She became paralyzed and blind, and felt something penetrate her head. In 1986, while reading her Bible on a couch, an alien suddenly appeared. Betty came out of her body and was taken to a strange place.

In 1987, a punch biopsy–like scoop mark appeared on the calf or her right leg. Three similar marks forming a triangle appeared on her right arm on August 14, 1988. I mention the specific date because on August 17, 1988, I received the same type scoop mark above the shin of my right leg. My personal physician was puzzled by its appearance and sent me to a dermatologist. He at first dismissed it as a recent punch biopsy and wondered why I had come to him. When I explained to him that I never had a punch biopsy, he, too, was puzzled. He told me that it looked like one and that the mark was made recently. I would add that these scoop marks are typically found by abductees after their abduction experience. The night before mine appeared, I dreamed that someone was operating on my leg!

The importance of bringing the Phase III experiences to the attention of UFO researchers and the public set me to writing yet another book about them. I entitled it *The Watchers.*[3] The revelation that other members of Betty's family were also being abducted in one way did not come as a surprise. The abduction phenomenon now is well known to be a *family affair* perhaps taking place over many generations. I hoped that, sometime in the future, I would be able to look into their experiences.

After the Phase III investigation, I knew that there was much left undone. During my earlier enquiry, Bob refused further hypnosis after reliving his 1944 and 1967 experiences. These memories had terrified him. In fall 1992, Bob finally agreed to be hypnotized. Betty and Becky (Betty's daughter) also were agreeable to hypnotic regression sessions so another follow-on investigation was launched.

Phase IV

Hypnosis sessions with Bob took place between November 6, 1992 and April 1994. The sessions with Betty, Bob, and Becky took place between November 1993 and February 1994. Summaries of their experiences follow.

Bob

Bob had written a letter to me about having a memory of being up in the sky looking down at scenery below him. Under hypnosis Bob remembered being in sixth grade in 1950. He was in bed, having stayed home from school because of a cold. He heard a buzzing sound and a light appeared in the darkened room. A small gray alien in red clothes appeared. He was taken out of his body and floated above the ground to a craft in the sky. They entered the craft through an opening in the bottom. He was returned the same way.

During follow-on sessions Bob remembered his mother telling him that she once saw a strange craft on the ground and remembered being inside. She was adamant about not being hypnotized. She did not want to know anything more about the incident. This was most interesting because Bob's next abduction experience included his mother and father. It took place at night from his bedroom. While awake, he heard his parents shut off their TV and suddenly found himself with his father in a strange, empty room. Then he spotted his mother. He watched as gray entities examined his parents. Then he remembered himself and his parents going down a dark hall, and he suddenly found himself back in bed.

Bob's next remembered encounter took place at night in winter 1989 at Laccochee, Florida, while visiting friends. He awoke suddenly when a bright red light shone through the bedroom window. His bed shook. One of the gray entities in a blue, skintight outfit appeared. Bob became very agitated. He could not move. The entity forced Bob to drink some liquid, which calmed him. He was then taken right through the wall to a craft. He was brought to a white, bright room and made to lie on a table. His eyes were examined by a pencil-shaped object that projected a bright, blue light. A helmet was placed on his head. It projected a picture of the earth with dark spots on the planet. They asked if he understood what this meant. Bob did not but was told that he would understand in time. He then was floated from the craft through the wall of his friend's house and placed back in bed.

Bob also told us about a dream that he had in 1993 where he was abducted to meet an alien-like *child*. When told to go back to the source of his dream, he found himself back in the craft where he had been abducted in 1967. During Bob's initial hypnosis he had forced himself not to remember several additional things that had occurred. One was that the red-suited entities had extracted sperm from Bob, which left a rash that his doctor could not explain. The other event was a strange-looking *child* being brought to him and being told that it was partly his.

"It was short.... He didn't have any hair...and had gray skin...and a little, small nose."

Bob became very emotional while gazing at the child. It looked at him longingly as if it wanted to go with Bob. Bob felt very sad when the aliens then took the child away.

Betty

During the November 6, 1992 hypnosis session Betty was drawn out of their trailer against her will. Outside she saw a large, hovering ball of blue light and suddenly found herself inside of it. Next she found herself in a room with three gray entities. One had a clear hood on his head. A similar hood was placed on Betty. It covered her head and shoulders. She was made to stand on a round area of the floor containing orifices. A liquid bubbled out of the orifices and filled the room. The hood allowed Betty and the alien to breathe. Betty found her head feeling heavier and heavier. The liquid emptied and Betty was brought to another room. A tiny blue light that had accompanied Betty initially appeared once again. The hood was removed and her head felt normal again. Betty was taken out of the craft with the blue light following her. It was misty outside. She was amazed to find herself back in the Crystal Forest that she had experienced during her abduction at age 13. Betty was placed in the large blue sphere again and taken to a landed round metal craft. She was told that she was going to be taken to a very *high place.*

It was a very high place. Betty was standing near a one-way window and saw a pitch-black sky dotted with tiny lights. The two aliens that accompanied Betty informed Betty that she was going to meet someone who wanted to talk with her. During the hypnosis session, Betty suddenly stopped talking and gasped. Even with her eyes closed, the expression on her face showed utter amazement. We wondered what in the world she was looking at. We soon found out that what she saw was definitely not in the world—far from it.

"Ah-h-h, it's a thing up in there in the darkness, and it's huge. Oh, we're coming up to something that is big—really, really big hanging in space. We're just moving closer and closer to this long thing."

Later, Betty drew a picture of what astonished her. It depicted a gigantic tube-shaped vessel floating against a jet-black backdrop punctuated by hundreds of stars. It dwarfed the craft that carried her! The huge ship had a metal-capped transparent enclosure in front that contained many red and white lights. Within the enclosure Betty could see three protruding, tongue-shaped tiers. The ship itself was girdled by three rotating rings.

As they approached the front of the craft, Betty described something that opened to let them in. She found it similar to the sectioned diaphragm that let out steam in an appliance used to steam vegetables. It reminded me of a camera's diaphragm that opened to let in light to expose film and then closed. Other small craft could be seen resting in indented bowl-like berths on the tiers. The craft Betty was in flew inside to rest in one of them.

Betty gazed in amazement out the one-way looking window. She saw a tall, human-like person with long white hair to his shoulders. He was dressed in a long white robe and approached the craft. This type of entity was called an Elder. She had seen such persons during her teenage experience just before she entered the Great Door to see The One. Betty was taken out of the craft and the tall, Nordic-appearing person called an Elder motioned the trio to follow him. Betty was surprised that she was actually walking, as usually she was floated along.

During her time in the huge mother ship, Betty learned the use of the red animals that she had seen in a red-lit enclosure during her 1967 experience. The worn-out eyes of the gray Watchers were replaced by newly grown eyes removed from the red creatures. She was also told that the tall Elders could see through the eyes of the gray Watchers, which were in effect living monitors for them.

Betty was privy to many sights on the huge mother ship. At one point she was shown a TV-like device, which had recorded a childhood scene from her past at church. She also witnessed a strange ceremony performed by Elders, a trip to earth with an Elder in an out-of-body state. There she saw how Elders secretly helped mankind while in this invisible state of being.

The crowning event of this particular abduction experience was being brought again to the Great Door and entering to see The One. But, again, the hypnotist was not able to persuade Betty to describe the beauty and love she experienced behind the door.

Afterward she was again placed in the round craft that had brought her to the mother ship. The craft returned to earth. Betty was placed back into the blue-glowing orb, which descended to the ground just outside the trailer. She entered and went to the bedroom where Bob was sleeping. She was shocked to the core when she saw her physical body in bed before she entered it. Betty had no idea how her physical body got back to the trailer while she was still in an OBE state of being.

A few other curious things were revealed under hypnosis. One involved a 1988 incident in their car while on their way home from a drive-in movie. For some reason they took a lonely route home. As they passed an apple orchard, something hit the car. A bright light enveloped it. Bob became paralyzed at the steering wheel. Amazed, Betty found that the car had been taken up into a craft into a large, open garage-like area. Another car was seen parked nearby. There appeared to be some kind of an altercation among some gray entities, which was dispersed by one of the tall robed Elders. Apparently they were not supposed to have been taken. They were returned to their car and later curious about the 45 minutes of missing time.

A 1989 abduction was most interesting because it involved Betty's daughter, Becky. Betty suddenly awoke and saw a multi-pronged object come through the window. It sprayed out streaks of light. Betty came out of her body and found herself beside a gray entity in a room aboard a craft. There, she was shocked to see Becky working at some kind of a console that had strange hieroglyphic-like writing on it. She rushed to Becky. When Betty's hand touched Becky, her hand passed right through her. An alien told Betty that they had been training Becky in "the letters" since she was a child but did not tell Betty why.

Betty was then placed in a blue sled-like machine, which traveled along a track. They disembarked and went into another room. On the way they passed a pie-shaped section, where Betty saw a naked woman lying on a table. She looked again and realized it was her own physical body lying there! The tall Elder had Betty enter her body. Betty was told that her physical body had been prepared for future OBE abductions. She was made to stand on a platform. Bright light surrounded her and she found herself back home in bed.

This ended our Part IV sessions with Betty and Bob. This session revealed that their children also were being abducted. As mentioned, several were seen being examined by small gray entities by Betty during her 1978 OBE abduction. This new information instigated an inquiry into what Betty's other family members may have experienced. Unfortunately, only Betty's daughter Becky agreed to undergo hypnosis. Other members of her and Bob's family refused. They wanted no part of an investigation.

Becky

The earliest hint of Becky having been abducted occurred when a neighbor knocked on Betty's door. She asked if she knew Becky was outside playing with no clothes on. Betty rushed outside and picked Becky up. She could not understand how Becky got out of her crib into the yard through a locked door. Also, she had diapered Becky before putting her to bed. Now she was naked. This event remained a mystery to Betty and later to Becky for years. A hypnosis probe was conducted on February 5, 1994. Becky was regressed to being in her crib that night. She relived what happened in detail. Brief excerpts from the session follow.

"It's, it's dark and there's light shining through and a pretty person (robed Elder) is there, smiling, looking at me....And I'm lifted up— held—I'm being held.... I'm going right up...like an elevator.... It's dark out...going toward the trees...and we're in a room.... There's a seat. It's, ah, like an L shape.... The pretty person *is sitting me down there and spraying me with air, misty air.... Putting on a T-shirt— looks like a T-shirt—getting down.... I'm walking over to my left."*

Becky was delighted to see that there were two other small children in that place with her: a little black girl who said her name was Nadine Freyberg, and a little boy who said his name was P.J.—Peter. The other children were playing with what seemed to be strange toys and bubble-like objects in the air. It was difficult to visualize the equipment that Becky was describing. Some had liquid inside, others whitish sand-like material, and others were clear, like Plexiglas.

The floating, glass-like bubbles had a hard surface and a little symbol could be seen inside them. However, her visit was for more than fun and games. One of the Elders placed an instrument, which tingled, on each of the children's ankles. Two other Elders arrived. Each carried a child to a section where they were surrounded by bright light. Becky found herself on the ground behind some bushes near her house.

It is interesting to note that Bob's son, Tony, and my younger brother Ricky were also found outside locked doors early in the morning by neighbors. In fact, the commonalities between our two families were so great that I made a detailed comparison between them in my last book, *The Andreasson Legacy.* However, this incident in Becky's life was just the beginning of multiple experiences with the alien entities. It was decided to discover if Becky had been abducted prior to this. There was still time to continue the session, and Becky was brought back to 1957 at age 2 1/2 when she lived in Westminster, Massachusetts. She was in a carriage in the yard and heard her name called three times. This seemed to be a prelude to what happened that night.

Again, Becky was in her crib. She heard a ticking noise just prior to the room being filled with light. A "pretty person" appeared and removed her pajamas and diaper. He placed her in his arms and both were elevated in light to a glowing craft. She found herself in a room where a bench like an ironing board came out from the wall. A human-like woman dressed in white appeared. She seemed familiar to Becky. The young woman had green eyes and curly hair. The woman sprayed her with a misty substance. Then something like a hat was placed upon her head, which made a whirring sound. Then her nightclothes were put back on and she was transported back to her crib.

When Becky was regressed to age 5, she remembered being taken care of by her grandfather, who told her that he had to leave her for a short time. Becky had never been left alone before and was very frightened, but remembered that a lady dressed in green had appeared to comfort her. Under hypnosis the woman told Becky that her name was Ishta. She held and rocked Becky in her arms, often walking to the window and looking out. She put Becky down and disappeared when Betty arrived to find Becky left alone. Betty was so upset with her father that she never let him babysit again.

The next strange encounter took place in 1961 when Becky was age 6. Becky was outdoors near some woods sitting on a favorite rock with some kittens when she heard her name being called. The same green-clothed woman named Ishta appeared. She smiled, lifted up Becky's left hand, and shone a bright light from a ring-like object on her finger onto Becky's finger. Then she turned and walked into the woods followed by two of the cats, which were never seen again. This was not the last appearance of Ishta.

At age 7, Becky walked to a pond and was dipping her bare feet in the water when she heard her voice being called. Abruptly, a circle of blue light struck the surface of the pond and began spreading out. A bluish object like a bubble appeared. When she reached out to touch it, she felt a painful tingling sensation. Becky quickly put her hand in the water and the object slipped off her finger. The blue light dissipated. Her finger was bleeding. She wiped it off and found a bump like a blister on it. Frightened, she started running home to tell her mother but strangely changed her mind and watched other kids playing nearby until the bleeding stopped.

One of the weirdest experiences suffered by Becky took place in 1962 at age 7. Under hypnosis, Becky recalled suddenly waking up at night and being floated out of bed inside a blue light. She was terrified to see a frightening dog-like creature in the corner of the room. A voice told her to stay in the beam of light. The light floated her downstairs and blinked out. She found herself in the dark and called for her mother. Betty brought Becky back to her room and showed her that there was nothing there. She sat with her for a while until Becky went back to sleep.

The next memory would be familiar to readers of *The Andreasson Affair*. Becky was regressed to age 11 and found herself at her South Ashburnham home in Massachusetts during the family's 1967 experience. She recalled the aliens bringing her out of suspended animation to see her mother with the gray entities. She remembered being kept conscious and left with one of the gray entities, named Jessup, during Betty's abduction. The gray being had Becky make a ball attached to a stick move by using her mind. Such mind games with children have been reported before.

Our probe into Becky's multi-faced experiences proved to be an embarrassment of riches. Like many other abduction reports, they seemed to be part of a never-ending story. She continued to report many inexplicable occurrences throughout her early life. At age 12, she remembered a number of experiences. She awoke to see a gray entity sitting on her brother Todd's bed. Another time she awoke to see a blue ball of light in her bedroom. At age 15, she was awakened by a blue light that shone on her and heard a voice telling her to remember some numbers. At age 16, she awoke to see a yellow-glowing entity by her bed that quickly disappeared. At age 20, she awoke to find herself paralyzed and one of the gray entities by her bed watching her. At age 24, she heard a buzzing noise that got louder and louder before a blue light shone into her room. She was told to step into it. When it started pulling her, she broke away from it and escaped into her sister's room. At age 29, she was terrified by blinking red eyes seen outside her bedroom window. At age 34, she awoke to find two entities at the foot of her bed. They pulled her leg out from under the covers and ran an egg-shaped instrument up and down her leg. It felt as if they were drawing a hot line from her foot, up to her knee on the inside of her leg. Then the two entities that reminded her of Quazgaa and Jessup turned and left right through the window.

The hypnosis sessions continued until 1995. Becky relived many experiences at ages 31, 33, 34, 38, and 39. These included abductions, apparitions, poltergeist phenomena, disembodied voices, and a phone call from a dead friend. But perhaps the most significant experiences were recalled during her regression at age 34. She revealed that she had been taken often by the gray entities to a "learning center." There she was taught on TV-like consoles to learn and write an unearthly language and how to measure light that exists in physical bodies. (Betty had observed Becky operating one of these consoles during an OBE abduction.) The OBE abductions of the Luca family instigated me to write yet another book: *The Watchers II*[4], which compared OBE abductions to OBES reported by persons during a near-death experience.

In closing, I should mention that Becky is continuing the otherworldly revelations first made public in *The Andreasson Affair.* She is co-hosting a hit radio show entitled *Supernatural Girlz* (*www.supernaturalgirlz.com*) with paranormal researcher Patricia Baker. The show airs every Saturday night from 9 to 11 p.m. EST and features interviews with leaders in the paranormal field.

In the meantime, other phenomena continue to haunt Betty and Bob, including the clock in their basement going backward, strange lights and symbols in their hallway and bedroom, and black unmarked helicopters flying over their home. Although retiring from the public eye in 1995, both have decided to go public with their experiences once again upon the publication of this newest edition of *The Andreasson Affair.*

Additional Biographical Data for Principals in the Andreasson Affair

Biographical data shown in the chart on page 234 was extracted from a tape-recorded interview with Betty Ann Andreasson on the afternoon of April 30, 1978, at the home of Raymond E. Fowler.

Establishing Witness Credibility

Nocturnal Light, Daylight Disc, Radar/Visual, and CE-I sightings all deal with witnesses who consciously see, remember, and report a UFO. Evidence for such reports is necessarily limited to a careful analysis of the witnesses' background and of their accounts.

CE-II's provide more than just anecdotal data to the investigator. In such cases, the visual sighting of a UFO is supported by supplementary evidences. This might include a recorded radar track that coincides with the location and maneuvers of a sighted UFO; a verifiable photographic image that corresponds with the eyewitness' description; and measurable ground effects left behind in a UFO's wake. Such supplementary evidence, when properly analyzed, aids in establishing the physical reality of a sighted UFO.

Close Encounters of the Fourth Kind sometimes present a problem when there is no supporting physical evidence and when, for some inexplicable reason, the witness's conscious memory has been blocked, as with

Name	Date of Birth (Date of Death)	Relationship	Hair Color	Eye Color	Height/Build
Waino Aho	July 27, 1906 (August 27, 1977)	Grandfather	Dark brown	Amber	5'10"/Large
Eva Aho	July 11, 1909	Grandmother	Black	Hazel	5'/Small
Waino Aho, Jr.	1930	Betty's brother			
Agnes Aho	1928	Waino's wife			
Shirley Rettberg	1928	Betty's sister			
Betty Andreasson	January 7, 1937	Mother	Black	Amber	5'4"/Medium
James Andreasson, Sr.	May 9, 1933	Father	Sandy blonde	Brown	6'2"/Large
Rebecca (Becky) Andreasson	May 8, 1955	Daughter	Strawberry blonde	Brown	5'2"/Medium
James Andreasson, Jr.	April 25, 1956 (October 23, 1977)	Son	Blonde	Blue	5'7"/Medium
Mark Andreasson	September 24, 1957	Son	Brown	Brown	5'8"/Medium
Scott Andreasson	February 16, 1959	Son	Dark brown	Dark brown	6'/Medium
Todd Andreasson	August 12, 1960 (October 23, 1977)	Son	Dark brown	Dark brown	5'10"/Medium
Bonnie Andreasson	April 10, 1962	Daughter	Golden brown	Brown	5'5"/Medium
Cindy Andreasson	December 9, 1963	Daughter	Blonde	Blue	5'7"/Medium

the Andreasson Affair. Such circumstances prohibit investigators from scientifically establishing that a real physical event took place as described.

Does this mean that such cases are not worth investigating? Not necessarily. There is a standard investigative procedure applicable to CE-IV cases such as the Andreasson Affair. It includes establishing witness credibility, extracting the forgotten experience through hypnosis, and, finally, thoroughly analyzing all collected data pertaining to the case at hand.

When analyzing and evaluating any given UFO sighting case, knowledge of the witnesses' character is essential. It is of special value when dealing with a single witness or with exceptionally bizarre reports. Alleged incidents involving UFO landings, the sighting of alien entities, communication with alien entities, abduction by alien entities, etc., are examples of cases exhibiting a high element of strangeness. In such cases, the background of the witnesses must be established.

Betty seems to have passed a relatively happy, secure, healthy childhood, as her tomboy ways would seem to suggest. She delighted in catching snakes, tadpoles, shiners, and trout: *"I remember going through the tunnel beneath our road with a barrel hoop and burlap sack attached to it, swishing a stick, as my friend Eddie stood at the other end with another hooded sack. We got more trout and snakes that way."* For sports, she enjoyed swimming, hiking, sliding, skating, basketball, hitting baseballs, football, and hunting. (Later in life, she still enjoyed playing on a woman's softball team.)

The Aho family lived variously in Fitchburg, Leominster, and Westminster, and Betty did fairly well at Westminster Elementary School. A check of the educational background of Betty Andreasson and her daughter Becky revealed that neither had fully completed high school, nor did they obtain special training of any kind. Becky married young, as had her mother, and had become equally engrossed in homemaking. Information was also sought concerning the witnesses' community reputation, attitudes, and personality traits.

In establishing the community reputation of a witness, one is basically concerned about honesty and basic human relations. Such information is obtained by questioning present friends, neighbors, teachers, ministers, and business associates. The principal witnesses—Betty and Becky—scored high in this category. The general impression gained was that they were "good neighbors," "very stable," and "honest," and that Betty was "hardworking," "dependable," "good mother," and "good homemaker." Each person questioned had no reason to doubt the witnesses' integrity.

The witnesses' attitudes—their philosophical beliefs and biases—were quite similar. Betty's parents were exceptionally devout people. Betty and her brother and sisters were raised in a home life centered around a vibrant Christian faith. Waino loved fishing, but both he and Eva devoted a great deal of time to studying the Bible. (Though he spoke English with no accent, he retained a command of his native Finnish.) They were both very active in the Pentecostal Church.

Shortly before she turned 17, Betty started attending the Pentecostal and Baptist churches. She did not smoke or drink—"could not stand the taste of beer or liquor"—but while in her teens, she had begun attending the Friday night dances at the local Youth Center.

Discovering her talent for jitterbugs and waltzes, she was briefly torn between a career in art or dance. Not until she was married and pregnant with her second child, James, Jr., did Betty give her "heart willingly over to Jesus and was born again, praise God!" The family initially lived in Westminster, renting Betty's father-in-law's house, where she pored over her Bible continuously. Later, she took pains to instill the same faith in her own children. Thus, both Betty and Becky could be classed as fundamentalist Christians who accept a very literal interpretation of the Bible and believe it to be the Word of God.

Such biases provide both potential strengths and weaknesses to the witnesses' credibility. On the one hand, experience has shown that such people are usually exceptionally honest. Interest in UFOs and paranormal phenomena are usually frowned upon by this wing of the Christian Church. On the other hand, a mystical person who interprets everything in terms of his or her preconceptions may not be an objective witness.

Nonetheless, Betty's powers of visual recall seemed unusually acute. Her husband, trained as a welder and pipe fitter, and able to read blueprints, was employed via Union Local 92 for many companies, such as Borden Chemical and Industrial Pipe of Leominster. On December 9,

1966, Betty was sitting in the family Volkswagen bus, waiting to pick up her husband's paycheck from the Catalytic Construction Company, when she witnessed a robbery of the union payroll.

Before jumping into the getaway car, one of the bandits ripped off his face mask, revealing a distinctive scar on his face. The robbers were shocked to realize that Betty had witnessed everything, but they drove off in a hurry without harming her. When police arrived, Betty was able to recall such details as the robbers' clothing, the interior of their car, and the license number, and her description led to the criminals' arrest in a matter of minutes.

Neither she nor Becky exhibited personality traits that would downgrade their credibility. Both were well dressed, orderly, courteous, and modest. Betty Andreasson voluntarily submitted to a psychiatric interview by a professional doctor, whose examination made no attempt to explore the reported UFO experience. Instead, he concentrated on Betty herself in order to establish an informal psychological profile. The doctor found no symptoms of active thought disorders or obvious psychiatric problems. He concluded that she believed in the reality of her experience. (It was his opinion, however, that her strong involvement in religion may have compromised her objectivity as a witness.)

Another investigative tool employed in establishing the credibility of the principal witnesses was the Psychological Stress Evaluator (PSE), an instrument developed by the Dektor Company[1] to detect, measure, and display certain stress-related components of the human voice.

When a person speaks, the human voice exhibits two types of modulation. The first type is that which we hear, and over which a person has conscious control. The second type, which cannot be heard, results from stress-related micro-muscle tremors that are beyond the control of the person who is speaking. In times of stress—especially when a person is deliberately lying—this second type of modulation disappears from the human voice. The greater the stress, the greater the suppressive effect on the micro-muscle tremors. The PSE graphically displays when this second modulation is missing or is being suppressed.

A PSE test consists of preparing a list of simple, selected questions, keyed to the person being tested. As in other sensor tests, like the polygraph or "lie detector," questions are selected to differentiate between normal, truthful answers and those that are blatantly false. In doing so, the test subject's voice pattern is firmly established. When compared to the norm, evasive or false answers reveal obvious stress patterns. It is important to note that the PSE has the ability to accept both narrative and yes/no answers from the test subject. The instrument is being used by law-enforcement officials, doctors, and lawyers, as well as by commercial organizations for pre-employment screening. In recent years, UFO investigators have enlisted the services of the professional PSE analyst as part of an overall inquiry into the credibility of certain UFO witnesses.

The PSE analysis was performed by Ernest C. Reid, a certified stress analyst. He has conducted (among others) a major security check of facilities at Atlanta International Airport in 1972, under the auspices of the Boston-based Interstate Detective Bureau.[2] PSE tests were administered to both Betty and Becky, during which many pertinent questions were asked about their alleged UFO experience. The analyst concluded that "they were telling the truth with regards to the 1967 incident." In his report (which included the results of the PSE test, inserted into the 528-page report sent to MUFON), Mr. Reid stated: "It is extremely unusual...that we would render an opinion as definitive as we would in this particular instance.... The seriousness of the situation...led us to analyze these charts with full respect for the rights of the subjects, the examiners and the validity of the instrumentation being used. In the opinion of this analyst, the results are conclusive."

Among the investigators, no one doubted that a UFO experience of some kind had occurred. Everyone felt that the witnesses were telling the truth as they knew it to be. Most believed that the witnesses' motives for reporting the event were pure (though a minority believed that the witnesses' motivation was financial gain—but following a real experience). A graphical representation of his PSE tests, with a listing of the questions and answers, is reproduced on the following pages.

The date is July 7, 1977. The time is 8 p.m. Eastern Daylight Time. The recording was made at the home of Jules Vaillancourt, 37 Williams Road, Ashburnham, Massachusetts. The equipment is a "Magnacord" with full-track heads run at 7 1/2 inches per second. The microphone is an "Electret" miniature. The questions are directed to Betty Ann Andreasson by Jules Vaillancourt, MUFON investigator. The recording tape used is virgin tape (600 feet on a five-inch reel) mylar base, Radio Shack part # 44-735.

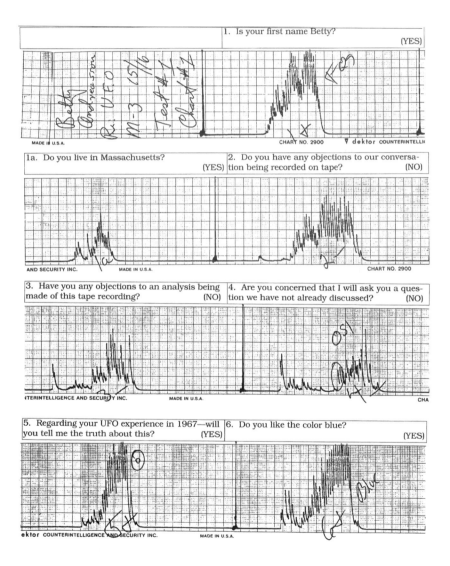

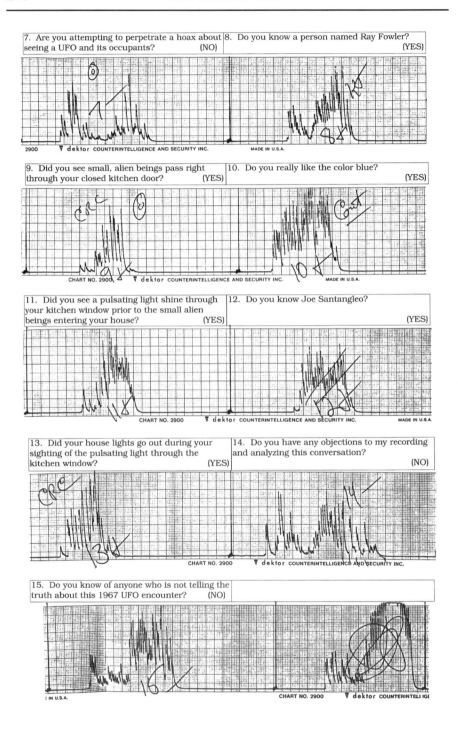

7. Are you attempting to perpetrate a hoax about seeing a UFO and its occupants? (NO)

8. Do you know a person named Ray Fowler? (YES)

2900 ▽ dektor COUNTERINTELLIGENCE AND SECURITY INC. MADE IN U.S.A.

9. Did you see small, alien beings pass right through your closed kitchen door? (YES)

10. Do you really like the color blue? (YES)

CHART NO. 2900 ▽ dektor COUNTERINTELLIGENCE AND SECURITY INC. MADE IN U.S.A.

11. Did you see a pulsating light shine through your kitchen window prior to the small alien beings entering your house? (YES)

12. Do you know Joe Santangleo? (YES)

CHART NO. 2900 ▽ dektor COUNTERINTELLIGENCE AND SECURITY INC. MADE IN U.S.A.

13. Did your house lights go out during your sighting of the pulsating light through the kitchen window? (YES)

14. Do you have any objections to my recording and analyzing this conversation? (NO)

CHART NO. 2900 ▽ dektor COUNTERINTELLIGENCE AND SECURITY INC.

15. Do you know of anyone who is not telling the truth about this 1967 UFO encounter? (NO)

IN U.S.A. CHART NO. 2900 ▽ dektor COUNTERINTELLIGI

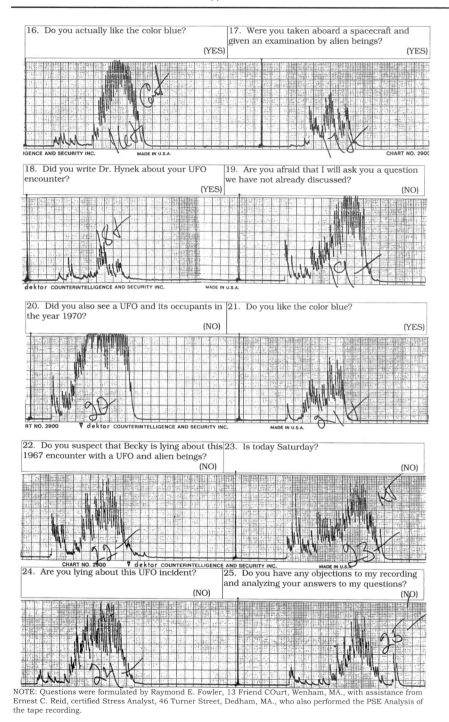

16. Do you actually like the color blue? (YES)

17. Were you taken aboard a spacecraft and given an examination by alien beings? (YES)

18. Did you write Dr. Hynek about your UFO encounter? (YES)

19. Are you afraid that I will ask you a question we have not already discussed? (NO)

20. Did you also see a UFO and its occupants in the year 1970? (NO)

21. Do you like the color blue? (YES)

22. Do you suspect that Becky is lying about this 1967 encounter with a UFO and alien beings? (NO)

23. Is today Saturday? (NO)

24. Are you lying about this UFO incident? (NO)

25. Do you have any objections to my recording and analyzing your answers to my questions? (NO)

NOTE: Questions were formulated by Raymond E. Fowler, 13 Friend COurt, Wenham, MA., with assistance from Ernest C. Reid, certified Stress Analyst, 46 Turner Street, Dedham, MA., who also performed the PSE Analysis of the tape recording.

Sample Questions Asked for PSE Test

Selected from 97 questions asked Betty and Becky Andreasson. Certain questions designed to establish a stress pattern are not included in this sample.

Question	Answer
Regarding your UFO experience in 1967	
Will you tell me the truth about this?	*Yes*
Are you attempting to perpetrate a hoax about seeing a UFO and its occupants?	*No*
Did you see small, alien beings pass right through your closed kitchen door?	*Yes*
Did you see a pulsating light shine through your kitchen window prior to the small alien beings entering your house?	*Yes*
Did your house lights go out during your sighting of the pulsating light through the kitchen window?	*Yes*
Do you know of anyone who is not telling the truth about this 1967 UFO encounter?	*No*
Were you taken aboard a spacecraft and given an examination by alien beings?	*Yes*
Do your drawings represent things or pictures that you actually saw during the 1967 UFO encounter?	*Yes*
Do you have any objections to my recording and analyzing this conversation?	*No*
Had you read about UFO abduction cases prior to your experience in 1967?	*No*
Had you heard about Betty and Barney Hill prior to your experience in 1967?	*No*
Has someone hypnotized you to make you believe the 1967 UFO experience really happened?	*No*
Did you make up a story about an experience with a UFO in 1967 from other stories that you have read about?	*No*

A·P·P·E·N·D·I·X B

➤ Rekindled Memories ◄

The combined results of the character checks and PSE tests had strongly established witness credibility. Our next step concerned extraction of the forgotten experience through hypnosis.

Although no one theory has explained the phenomenon of hypnosis to the satisfaction of all researchers, its existence has been known for thousands of years. In the past, it was largely confined to the occult, parlor games, and the stage. In recent years, however, it has found practical usage among doctors, dentists, and criminologists. One of its applications involves the recall of memories repressed or forgotten by the conscious mind. Thus, it is a logical tool for cases such as the Andreasson Affair.

Psychiatrist Benjamin Simon, MD, used hypnotic regression to help Betty and Barney Hill consciously recall their missing hours. Author John G. Fuller documented the results in *The Interrupted Journey,* and in the introduction to this fascinating book, Dr. Simon made an interesting statement:

> Hypnosis is a useful procedure in psychiatry to direct concentrated attention on some particular point in the course of the whole therapeutic procedure. In cases like the Hills', it can be the key to the locked room, the amnesic period. Under hypnosis, experiences buried in amnesia may be recalled in much shorter time than in the normal course of psychotherapeutic process.[1]

Dr. Simon stressed that hypnosis was not necessarily a magical road to truth: "In one sense this is so, but it must be understood that hypnosis is a pathway to truth as it is felt and understood by the...participant. The truth is *what he believes to be the truth*. This may or may not be consonant with the ultimate truth. *Most frequently it is*."[2]

Since the Hills' UFO experience in 1961, hypnosis has been used by a number of UFO researchers, especially when investigating CE-IVs. The most prominent of these researchers is Dr. R.L. Sprinkle of the University of Wyoming and consultant in psychology to the Aerial Phenomena Research Organization (APRO).[3] Dr. Sprinkle has written:

> Further emphasis should be given to the uses of hypnotic time regression procedures for investigation of UFO experiences. An exciting possibility exists that these procedures can provide more information about these *loss of time* experiences, including possible cases of abduction and examination by UFO occupants. Hypnotic procedures can be used to assist UFO witnesses in decreasing anxiety and gaining more confidence in the (personal) reality of their experiences; further, these procedures can be helpful to UFO investigators by providing them with more information about UFO witnesses and their unusual experiences. Further studies may lead to an outline or pattern of UFO abduction cases and the significance of these experiences in understanding the puzzle of UFO phenomena.[4]

It was with these thoughts in mind that Becky and Betty were brought to the offices of the New England Institute of Hypnosis directed by Harold Edelstein, our local MUFON hypnosis consultant. On May 8, 1978, the Boston *Herald American* newspaper ran a front-page story on Dr. Edelstein's involvement in police investigation. The article, written by staff writer Laura White, is worth quoting from because it aptly illustrates how hypnosis is being used in the investigative process:

> Twenty police officers, some with service revolvers and handcuffs dangling from their belts, sat in the classroom at Pine Manor Junior College eyeballing the goateed man standing before them.

Dr. Harold Edelstein was going to introduce the seasoned officers to a new investigative technique: Hypnosis...is a relatively new tool for local police. Methuen police detective Bill Rayno was introduced to hypnosis last May and used it on a case that was at a standstill after two years investigation. Three Combat Zone prostitutes had been found murdered north of Boston, one in Rayno's jurisdiction.

"We'd exhausted all leads," admits Rayno. "Then a witness agreed to hypnosis and was able to recall time and details of a vehicle seen in the area where one of the victims had disappeared." Today, Rayno is working on new leads.... During the Chowchilla kidnapping investigation in 1976, the driver of the school bus underwent hypnosis and recalled the descriptions of the three abductors, their van and five of the six numbers on the van's license plate. California, Oregon, and Alaska courts have ruled information obtained under hypnosis as admissible.

...The key to hypnosis is developing a bond of confidence between the subject and hypnotist. Edelstein doesn't use the stereotypical swinging pendulum to put a subject in a "trance." Instead, he prefers to have a subject concentrate on a focal point about eyelevel as he counts backwards from five. At the numeral one, the subject's eyes are closed. Then Edelstein begins a monotone series of suggestions to relax the muscles in the body starting with the head. "By the time the whole body is relaxed, the subject should be ready to respond to commands," said Edelstein.

...For witnesses or victims who might be traumatized by recalling an event blotted out of their consciousness, Edelstein advises police to use the hypnotic suggestion of viewing events through a TV screen. "He feels like a spectator of what occurred instead of having been 'personally involved,'" says detective Rayno.... "Hypnosis doesn't put you in a trance," said Sgt. Sid Goodman, of the Boston Police Academy, an early student of Edelstein's.... John Peters, staff executive to the Braintree Police Chief...says hypnosis aids officers to relax, build confidence, heighten sensitivities, and lower anxieties.... Apparently, police departments around the state agree with Peters. Wednesday, 23 detectives will begin Massachusetts Training Council classes in hypnosis conducted by Dr. Edelstein at the Braintree Police Academy.

Dates of Hypnotic/Debriefing Sessions
Extracted from Volume I, Section V, pp. 1, 2 of
UFO Report CE-III/MA-77 (67-41A)

Session	Date
1	April 3, 1977
2	April 9, 1977
3	April 23, 1977
4	April 30, 1977
5	May 7, 1977
6	May 14, 1977
7	May 21, 1977
8	June 4, 1977 (Ray Fowler begins attending.)
9	June 18, 1977
10	June 23, 1977
11	June 26, 1977
12	July 16, 1977 (Dave Webb begins attending.)
13	July 23, 1977
14	July 28, 1977

A·P·P·E·N·D·I·X C

➤ Fred Youngren's Reconstructions ≺

Betty's artistic ability, coupled with a vivid hypnotic recall of the experience, enabled her to reconstruct the bizarre episode pictorially. Some of the remarkable drawings reproduced earlier in this book depicted the physical appearance of her captors. We decided to go a step further. In early June 1977, plans were made to attempt to construct a three-dimensional head and shoulder bust of Quazgaa.

Because Fred Youngren's daughter, Faith, was skilled in the art of sculpting, she was asked to perform this task. Betty's drawings were employed as an initial guide in the preparation of a preliminary model. This was completed late in June. Soon after, Fred visited Betty at her home in Ashburnham to obtain her comments. Betty recommended changes be made to the eyes and to the cheek contour.

On July 16, Quazgaa's evolving head was unceremoniously carried to session 12 in a mop bucket for further examination and suggested modifications by Betty. Fred performed the necessary changes during the session, with Betty's guidance and final approval. By the next session, Fred had been able to make a hollow rubber mold from which he would be able to cast a number of plaster duplicates. A plaster outer mold was constructed to support the rubber mold.

By the end of July, plaster casts of the model began rolling off the assembly line. Sandpaper applied in the correct places shaped and smoothed the tiny busts in preparation for painting, the final step that would transform each into the fetus-like, staring image of Quazgaa.

Fred experimented with a number of shades of gray spray paint in order to obtain the right color and *wet* look for the skin. Obtaining the proper color of blue for the suit also was a problem. Finally, by the end of August, all colors had been selected and approved by Betty. A total of 12 busts were carefully painted. Betty, Becky, and each of the principal investigators were given one. It was an apt memento of the strangest case that I have ever investigated.

In addition, Fred Youngren discovered that the various rooms and corridors logically fit within an object of the size and shape Betty had described. (See Figure 11 on page 48.)

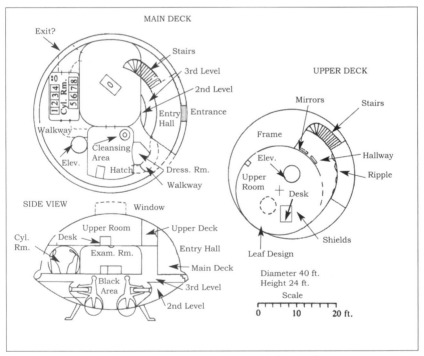

Figure 41: *Fred R. Youngren's reconstruction of the craft. Drawn December 28, 1977.*

In his final report, Fred stated: "The internal consistency in the sketches that Mrs. Andreasson made for us over a period of months is great and provides them with a degree of self-validation. Even more important, however, is the fact that the combination of these sketches into a *coherent* craft has produced a powerful corroboration of the witness' account."

It should be noted, however, that Fred's drawing assumes that Betty remained in the *same* craft. If she boarded a smaller vehicle that ascended and merged with a larger craft, Betty would have thought she was merely moving from one room to another within the same vehicle.

There are some hints of this—first, Betty's description of the size of the craft in the backyard retrieved under hypnosis during session three on April 23, 1977. When field investigator Jules Vaillancourt asked Betty, "How big is the ship?" Betty replied, "It looks small." A craft of the size drawn by Fred would have just barely fit behind Betty's former house and would have been very conspicuous; thus, it is more logical to assume that Betty boarded a small shuttle craft.

Betty recalled the craft that she initially entered as a small room with curved walls. Upon entering, she felt weightless ("I feel weightless and icky") for a considerable time ("I'm tired of just standing there"). It could very well be that during this time, Betty was experiencing the effects of rapid acceleration upward to rendezvous with larger craft containing chambers of the size and dimensions pictured by Fred Youngren. Betty then would have been examined, placed in the liquid-filled chair, and brought to the alien place by this larger raft.

A·P·P·E·N·D·I·X D

≻ A Fifth Entity? ≺

The Andreasson case is an ongoing investigation. There are bits and pieces that we are still trying to fit together. Dr. Edelstein warned us that once the basic event was remembered via hypnosis we could expect further things to be remembered. And indeed, over the months, both Betty and Becky have been experiencing flashbacks of memory of segments of the event that we had not explored in the report.

For example, the possibility exists that a total of *five* (not four) aliens initially entered the Andreasson home. One alien may have stayed behind to watch over Betty's family during her abduction.

This conjecture is based upon some curious and previously unresolved statements Betty and Becky made during the hypnotic regression sessions, and also by Betty in her initial correspondence to Dr. Hynek. In this letter, Betty stated that she thought a total of "five beings in all" had entered her house. We sought to confirm this during the second hypnosis session on April 9, 1977. Let us now go back in time hypnotically to the time when Betty first saw the entities enter her home through the kitchen door.

Betty: As they came through the door, it was like form after form after form.

Harold: How many?

Betty: Four, I think.

Harold: I want you actually to look at them and count them as you look
           at them.

Betty: One, one—they're kind of directly behind each other, so it—
           there's one, two, three, four, but it seems—

Harold: Are you sure there's only four, and not five?

Betty: It seems as if—there's—you know how steam is left behind?
           That's still there.

Harold: Is that another being, or isn't it?

Betty: I don't think it's another being. I think it's vapor.

Later, when Betty led the aliens from the kitchen into the living room
to show them the Bible, she noticed that this "vaporous form" accompanied the entities.

Betty: The Bible was right there on the end table.

Joseph: Did you hand this to the leader?

Betty: Yes, I took that—the leader came in, and the others came in
           with him, and they stood at an angle to the right of him, and I—

Harold: When they stood at an angle to the right of him, they're all in
           view? Am I correct?

Betty: Yeah, they're all in view.

Harold: I want you to look at them and count them, and tell me how
           many there are.

Betty: There's something strange there all the time because there
           seems to be a "shade" [a dark shape] or something I can't make
           out. I don't know if it stands directly in back of the leader, or
           what it is. It seems to be a shade or something. I don't know.

Under hypnosis, as it turned out, Betty could only see *four* entities in
the kitchen and the living room at any one time. *Four* accompanied her to
the craft. To further add to her confusion, when she entered the craft into
the half-bubble-shaped room, there were a total of five. One was probably already in there waiting for them. She was very puzzled about this.

Recent memory flashbacks during the ongoing investigation paralleling the writing of this book have provided further information on this matter. Later, during a memory flashback to her experience, she came to believe that a *fifth* alien in the group had entered the house through the kitchen door. During an interview on June 8, 1978, Betty was asked to sum up her thoughts about this for the record.

Betty: When they [aliens] came in, remember Dr. Edelstein kept on telling me, "Count them"? There was an additional one, but he disappeared over to the side. Remember the *shadow?*

Jules: Yeah, we thought it might be the mist.

Betty: The vapor? But it was *his* vapor, *his* slot, *his* place, or whatever. I just saw them come through, and I knew there were five, but it was confusing because when they were standing there, there were four. When Dr. Edelstein kept on about counting them, I knew I had seen five, but I only counted four, and then there was a form [the shade] and this troubled me for a long time, you know? The *form* behind Quazgaa. There was a *form* there, not a person, but a *slot*. The other being had gone where my father was.

In other words, Betty thinks the "shade" was the vacated slot that the fifth entity had traveled in and that she had entered when she moved out of the house with the other aliens.

See, what happened was, the *other* being stayed in the house. A lot of different things are coming back, and I was mentioning it to Becky. She says that for months now, things have come back to her and there *was* a being left behind in the house.

Under hypnosis, Becky had originally told us that when she woke up temporarily from suspended animation, she saw her mother looking at the blue book with the aliens. Then she remembered waking up in bed the next morning. However, she also remembered seeing one of the aliens holding a white glowing ball of light; at that time, she could not recall when.

I had assumed that she must have awakened briefly when one of the aliens with the glowing ball put her to bed. This made sense because during session 11, on June 26, 1977, as Betty described her family's state after being returned to her house, she seemed to describe Becky's brief awakening.

Betty: And they're still all sitting there motionless. Becky's sitting there and she's smiling and grinning. She seems to be *awake*— she's up, standing up, just smiling at me. [Then, abruptly, Becky's facial muscles stiffened again.] Oh-h-h [*Softly*]— Her expression isn't changing now. She seems *frozen* in that smile. Just standing up there in the living room.

Over the months following the hypnotic sessions, Becky began recalling some very interesting things. Apparently, one of the aliens was left behind as a babysitter for the family during Betty's absence! During a follow-up interview on June 8, 1978, investigator Jules Vaillancourt made a tape recording of Becky's account:

Becky: It kept on popping up in my mind—that there was a being in the house that stayed there when Mom and all the other beings left. I was thinking, "That can't be, because they all went out with Mom. So how could there have been one with me and the kids and grandparents?" I couldn't believe it was true. During daily chores, it kept reoccurring and reoccurring in my mind and bugging me. There was a being that stayed there because he was talking with me. I took him through the house to show him the rooms where everybody slept and one room I was afraid to go in, which was the cellar.

They did not go into the cellar.

Jules: What did he look like? Was he similar to Quazgaa, or was he like the other three?

All the beings were identical in appearance except for Quazgaa, who as a bit taller.

Becky: No, he was like the other three. He was shorter and he was showing me balls of light in the air. Like, he—you know, if you played tic-tac-toe on the ground, right? Well, he made it up in the air, and balls of light were going wherever he made them—like a juggler. He was showing me games, a lot of new things. It was a good feeling. I was having a lot of fun. I wasn't even afraid of the dark.

Apparently, the alien kept Becky awake only long enough to obtain certain information about the house, during which time he kept her happy by amusing her with the lights in the air.

Becky: It didn't seem very long, and I saw my brothers and sisters on the couch and everything.

Jules: What were they doing?

Becky: Just sitting there.

Jules: Were they moving around?

Becky: No, but they had a—um—when they were just sitting there, they had a very peaceful, non-afraid—something I can't explain— so that there was no fear connected with looking at them, you know, frozen like that. Then, ah, besides the games, one time I was going to *talk*—I had been talking through mind telepathy, and I went to speak out a word audibly. And when I did, the word "warbled." It went *whrew-whrew-whrew,* and it startled me. He put his hand on my shoulder and I wasn't afraid anymore. I just continued to talk through the mind.

If an entity were indeed left behind during Betty's absence, it would help explain a certain strange occurrence she had reported upon her return. When Betty was with the aliens, she obviously was under some type of mind control and did not remember that there had been an alien left behind in the house. During the hypnosis session covering the period of time, when she returned with her two companions, Betty never specifically stated that she saw three entities in the house. She did, however, make some puzzling statements in a portion of session eleven (June 26, 1977). Betty was in the living room, watching one of the two aliens going out the door with her children to bring them to bed. Her other companion stood silently beside her. Suddenly, she was startled to find another alien being standing beside her!

Betty: Oh! That other one is just suddenly in front of me. *I didn't even see him come in.* He's just there.

Betty assumed that this was the same being that had left the room with her children. But she had not seen him re-enter the living room. He could have come in another door, but it would have meant walking way out of his way around the house. Interestingly enough, the same thing occurred when this being left the room with her mother and father. Again, Betty seemed to be left in the room with just one alien. However, no sooner had he left than Betty stated: "And suddenly that one is in front of me again!"

Was Betty unknowingly involved with *three* instead of *two* aliens? This would make it seem as if the second being kept appearing out of nowhere. If not, where was the *third* entity that both Betty and Becky think remained behind to guard the family? Had he returned to the ship after his two companions came back with Betty? Are Betty and Becky experiencing a true recall of events, or are their minds playing tricks on them? Because both Betty and Becky were in bed when the aliens left the house, we'll probably never know.

> Notes <

Chapter 1

1. CUFOS, 1609 Sherman Ave., Suite 207, Evanston, Ill., 60201.
2. NICAP, 3535 University Blvd., Suite 23, Kensington, Md., 20795.
3. John Fuller, *Incident at Exeter* (New York: G. P. Putnam's Sons, 1966).
4. MUFON, 103 Oldtowne Rd., Seguin, Tex., 78155.
5. Directed by Ted Bloecher, 317 E. 83rd St., New York, N.Y., 10028, and David Webb, 64 Jacqueline Rd., Waltham, Mass., 02154.
6. John G. Fuller, *The Interrupted Journey* (New York: Dial Press, 1966).
7. New England Institute of Hypnosis, 544R Salem St., Wakefield, Mass., 01180.

Chapter 2

1. Despite Betty's use of "Quazgar" on her drawings, we arrived at the spelling of "Quazgaa" for our report. In hypnosis session seven, Betty tried to spell his name phonetically and said, "I see a Z, A, A. Big Z, A, Z." Nobody really picked up on this, unfortunately, and all of us, including Betty, pronounced and spelled the name with an "R" sound at the end. Later, when we began writing the final report, we referred to the transcript and checked with Betty. We finally agreed that "Quazgaa" best reflected the correct phonetic spelling.

Chapter 6

1. *Collier Encyclopedia,* 1967, s.v. "Phoenix."
2. Ibid.

Chapter 11

1. *APRO Bulletin*, July 1964, p. 8.
2. Ibid., March 1977, pp. 1, 7.
3. *Central Coast Express,* Gosford NSW, Australia, November 14, 1974.
4. *MUFON UFO Journal,* February 1977, p. 3.
5. Anne-Marie Strickland, *Sunday Mail*, Adelaide, Australia.
6. Pat Patrick, *Lubbock Avalanche Journal,* Lubbock, Texas, June 25, 1977.
7. *International UFO Reporter*, December 1977, pp. 4, 8.
8. *APRO Bulletin,* September–October 1967, p. 11.
9. NICAP, *The UFO Evidence,* VIII (E-M Cases), pp. 74, 75.
10. Major Donald G. Carpenter, *Introductory Space Science,* Vol. II. (1968), p. 461.
11. David Webb, *An Analysis of the Fall 1973 UFO/Humanoid Wave* (Evanston, Ill.: Center for UFO Studies, 1976), p. 52.
12. Gordon Lore, *Strange Effects from UFOS,* NICAP Special Report, 1969, p. 24.
13. Raymond E. Fowler, *UFOs: Interplanetary Visitors* (New York: Exposition Press, 1974), p. 324.
14. Lore, *Strange Effects,* pp. 61, 62.
15. Major Donald E. Keyhoe, USMC (Ret.), and Gordon Lore, *UFOs: A New Look* NICAP, 1969, p. 30.
16. Raymond E. Fowler, *UFOs: Interplanetary Visitors* (New York: Exposition Press, 1974), p. 323.
17. All quotations in this section from John G. Fuller, *The Interrupted Journey.*
18. IEE Spectrum, "Communication With Extraterrestrial Intelligence," March 1966, pp. 161–62.
19. Youngren's annotated drawings are included in Appendix C.
20. *UFO Investigator,* NICAP, May–June 1967, p. 6.

Chapter 12

1. Coral and Jim Lorenzen, *Abducted* (New York: Berkley Publishing Corporation, 1977) p. 58.

2. "Studying Wildlife by Satellite," *The National Geographic*, January 1973, pp. 120–23.

3. John G. Fuller, *The Interrupted Journey.*

Epilogue

1. Raymond E. Fowler, *The Andreasson Affair—Phase Two* (N.J.: Prentice-Hall, Inc., 1982; Tigard, Oreg.: Wildflower Press, 1994).

2. Raymond E. Fowler, *The Andreasson Legacy* (New York: Marlowe and Company, 1997).

3. Raymond E. Fowler, *The Watchers* (New York: Bantam Books, 1990, 1991).

4. Raymond E. Fowler, *The Watchers II* (Tigard, Oreg.: Wildflower Press, 1995).

Appendix A

1. Dektor Counterintelligence and Security, Inc., P.O. Box 238, Linwood, N.J., 08221.

2. Robert L. Ward, Boston *Evening Globe,* March 9, 1972.

Appendix B

1. New York: Dial Press, 1966, p. xi.

2. Ibid. Emphasis added.

3. APRO, 3910 E. Kleindale Rd., Tucson, Ariz., 85712.

4. Coral and Jim Lorenzen, *Abducted,* p. 216.

➤ Bibliography ◄

Books

Carpenter, Major Donald G. *Introductory Space Science* (United States Air Force Academy, 1968).

"Electro-Magnetic (E-M) Effects," *The UFO Evidence* (Washington, D.C.: National Investigations Committee on Aerial Phenomena, 1964).

Fowler, Raymond E., ed. *Field Investigator's Manual* (Seguin, Tex.: Mutual UFO Network, 1975).

———. *UFOs: Interplanetary Visitors* (New York: Exposition Press, 1974).

Fuller, John G. *Incident at Exeter* (New York: G.P. Putnam's Sons, 1966).

———. *The Interrupted Journey* (New York: Dial Press, 1966).

Graham, Billy. *Angels: God's Secret Agents* (New York: Doubleday, 1975).

Hall, Richard H., ed. "Electro-Magnetic (E-M) Effects," *The UFO Evidence* (Washington, D.C.: National Investigations Committee on Aerial Phenomena, 1964).

Hynek, J. Allen. *The UFO Experience: A Scientific Inquiry* (Chicago, Ill.: Henry Regnery, 1972).

Keel, John. *Why UFOs?* (New York: Manor Books, Inc., 1970).

Keyhoe, Major Donald E., USMC (Ret.), and Gordon Lore. *UFOs: A New Look* (Washington, D.C.: National Investigations Committee on Aerial Phenomena, 1969).

Lore, Gordon. *Strange Effects from UFOs* (Washington, D.C.: National Investigations Committee on Aerial Phenomena, 1969).

Lorenzen, Coral E. *Abducted: Confrontations With Beings From Outer Space (A Berkley Medallion Book)* (New York: Berkely Publishing Corporation, 1977).

Shklovskii, I.S., and Carl Sagan. *Intelligent Life in the Universe* (San Francisco, Calif.: Holden-Day, Inc., 1966).

Sullivan, Walter. *We Are Not Alone* (New York: McGraw-Hill Book Company, 1964).

Webb, David. *An Analysis of the Fall 1973 UFO/Humanoid Wave* (Evanston, Ill.: Center for UFO Studies, 1976).

Periodicals and Articles

A.P.R.O. Bulletin, Aerial Phenomena Research Organization, Tucson, Ariz., 1954–1978.

"Communication With Extraterrestrial Intelligence," *IEE Spectrum*, March 1966.

Forkey, Shelby. "Westminster Crash Kills Two Brothers," *Sentinel and Enterprise*, Fitchberg-Leominster, Mass., October 24, 1977.

Herald Journal, Syracuse, N.Y., December 21, 1967.

International UFO Reporter, Center for UFO Studies, Evanston, Ill., 1976–1978.

MUFON UFO Journal, Mutual UFO Network, Seguin, Tex., 1969–1978.

O Dia, Brazil, April 22, 1976.

Patrick, Pat. "Cigar-Shaped Object," *Lubbock Avalanche Journal*, Lubbock, Tex., June 25, 1977.

"Studying Wildlife by Satellite," *The National Geographic*, January 1973.

"Television," *The Patriot Ledger*, January 25, 1967.

UFO Investigator, National Investigations Committee on Aerial Phenomena, Washington, D.C./Kensington, Md., 1957–1978. (NICAP moved to Kensington in 1973.)

"UFO Sighting," *Central Coast Express*, Gosford NSW, Australia, November 14, 1974.

White, Laura, "Hypnosis: Latest Tool in Police Investigation," *Herald American*, Boston, Mass., May 8, 1978.

Reports/Records (PersonalFiles)

Fowler, Raymond E. *The Andreasson UFO Report*, 3 vols., South Ashburnham, Mass.

———. UFO Report No. 64-6, Lynn, Mass.

———. UFO Report No. 67-2, Boxford, Mass.

———. UFO Report No. 67-4, Williamstown, Mass.

————. UFO Report No. 67-5, Methuen, Mass.

————. UFO Report No. 67-9, Amherst, Mass.

————. UFO Report No. 67-11, Andover, Mass.

————. UFO Report No. 67-12, Dorchester, Mass.

————. UFO Report No. 67-13, Marlboro, Mass.

————. UFO Report No. 67-18, Leominster, Mass.

————. UFO Report No. 67-19, Andover, Mass.

————. UFO Report No. 67-20, Phillipston, Mass.

————. UFO Report No. 67-28, Royalston, Mass.

————. UFO Report No. 67-29, Orange, Mass.

————. UFO Report No. 67-30, Tully, Mass.

————. UFO Report No. 67-31, Orange, Mass.

————. UFO Report No. 67-35, Phillipston, Mass.

————. UFO Report No. 67-35B, Confidential, Mass.

————. UFO Report No. 67-36, Orange, Mass.

————. UFO Report No. 67-44B, Newton, Mass.

Municipal Light Company. *Work Sheet Records*, Ashburnham, Mass., January 25, 26, 1967.

Steward, M.C. (observer). U.S. Dept. of Commerce-Weather Bureau, *Record of River and Climatological Observations* (Station: Ashburnham, Mass.), January–March, 1967.

Letters

Andreasson, Betty Ann. To J. Allen Hynek, dated August 20, 1975, at Ashburnham, Mass.

➤ Index ➤

➢ About the Author ➤

Raymond E. Fowler was born in Salem, Massachusetts, and received a BA *magna cum laude* from Gordon College of Liberal Arts. His career included a tour with the USAF Security Service and 25 years with GTE Government Systems. He retired early after working as a task manager and senior planner on several major weapons systems including the Minuteman and MX Intercontinental Ballistic Missiles.

Raymond E. Fowler.

Ray Fowler's contributions to Ufology are respected by UFO researchers throughout the world. His investigation reports have been published in congressional hearings, military publications, newspapers, magazines, and professional journals in the United States and abroad. The USAF UFO Projects' Chief Scientific Consultant, Dr. J. Allen Hynek, has called Raymond Fowler, "An outstanding UFO investigator.... I know of none who is more dedicated, trustworthy or persevering." Ray served as chairman of the NICAP

Massachusetts Subcommittee, an early warning coordinator for the USAF-contracted UFO Study at the University of Colorado, and as a scientific associate for the Center for UFO Study. In later years he served as director of investigations on the board of directors of the Mutual UFO Network (MUFON).

He also has appeared on hundreds of radio/TV shows in the United States since 1963, including Dave Garroway, Dick Cavett, Mike Douglas, *Good Morning America, Unsolved Mysteries, Sightings,* and a number of network and syndicated documentaries on UFOs.

Ray has written 10 books on the subject of UFOs: *UFOs: Interplanetary Visitors, The Andreasson Affair, The Andreasson Affair-Phase Two, Casebook of a UFO Investigator, The Melchizedek Connection, The Watchers, The Allagash Abductions, The Watchers II, The Andreasson Legacy,* and *UFO Testament.*

Ray also is an amateur astronomer and teacher. He built Woodside Planetarium & Observatory and directed its operations between 1970 and 2001. During this time he presented adult and children's star shows supplemented by observation sessions with a 14-inch Schmidt-Cassegrain telescope. He sponsored a variety of courses himself and for local community colleges: UFO Seminar, The UFO Abduction Phenomenon, Mystery Phenomena, The Near Death Experience, Astronomy for Beginners, Astronomy with Binoculars and Small Telescopes, Cosmology for Beginners, Fresh Water Fishing, Vegetable Gardening, and children's courses in astronomy and fresh-water fishing. Ray moved to Kennebunk, Maine, in 2002 and continues teaching and lecturing.